T0293803

ROUTLEDGE LIBRARY EDITIONS:
MANAGEMENT

Volume 14

THE NEW MANAGEMENT CHALLENGE

THE NEW MANAGEMENT CHALLENGE

Information Systems for Improved Performance

Edited by
DAVID BODDY, JAMES MCCALMAN
AND DAVID A. BUCHANAN

LONDON AND NEW YORK

First published in 1988 by Croom Helm Ltd

This edition first published in 2018
by Routledge
2 Park Square, Milton Park, Abingdon, Oxon OX14 4RN

and by Routledge
711 Third Avenue, New York, NY 10017

Routledge is an imprint of the Taylor & Francis Group, an informa business

British Library Cataloguing in Publication Data
A catalogue record for this book is available from the British Library

ISBN: 978-1-138-55938-7 (Set)
ISBN: 978-1-351-05538-3 (Set) (ebk)
ISBN: 978-1-138-56455-8 (Volume 14) (hbk)
ISBN: 978-1-315-12257-1 (Volume 14) (ebk)

Publisher's Note
The publisher has gone to great lengths to ensure the quality of this reprint but points out that some imperfections in the original copies may be apparent.

Disclaimer
The publisher has made every effort to trace copyright holders and would welcome correspondence from those they have been unable to trace.

THE NEW MANAGEMENT CHALLENGE

Information Systems for Improved Performance

Edited by
DAVID BODDY, JAMES McCALMAN AND
DAVID A. BUCHANAN

CROOM HELM
London ● New York ● Sydney

© 1988 David Boddy, James McCalman and David Buchanan
Croom Helm Ltd, Provident House,
Burrell Row, Beckenham, Kent BR3 1AT
Croom Helm Australia, 44–50 Waterloo Road,
North Ryde, 2113, New South Wales

Published in the USA by
Croom Helm
in association with Methuen, Inc.
29 West 35th Street
New York, NY 10001

British Library Cataloguing in Publication Data

The new management challenge: information
    systems for improved performance.
    1. Management information systems —
    Data processing
    I. Boddy, David II. McCalman, James
    III. Buchanan, David A.
    658.4′038′0285   T58.6

    ISBN 0-7099-5084-5

Library of Congress Cataloging-in-Publication Data

The New management challenge: information systems for improved
    performance/edited by David Boddy James McCalman, and David A.
    Buchanan.
        p.   cm. — (UWIST/Croom-Helm management and new technology
    series)
        Bibliography: p.
        Includes index.
        ISBN 0-7099-5084-5
        1. Management information systems. I. Boddy, David.
    II. McCalman, James. III. Buchanan, David A. IV. Series:
    UWIST/Croom Helm series on management and new information
    technology.
    T58.6.N48   1988
    658.4′038 — dc 19   87-30610
                                                             CIP

Filmse by Mayhew Typesetting, Bristol, England
Printed and bound in Great Britain
by Billing & Sons Limited, Worcester.

Contents

List of Figures and Tables

Contributors

Alan Arthurs is in the School of Management, University of Bath. Current research interests are: the industrial relations consequences of the decline in manual work; work discipline; and equal pay for work of equal value. He is the National Co-ordinator of the ESRC Open Door Scheme and an Independent Expert in Equal Pay.

David Boddy is Reader in Management Studies at the University of Glasgow Business School, Centre for Technical and Organisational Change. He has written widely on the management aspects of computing and information technology and is currently directing a study of the management of convergent technologies.

David A. Buchanan is Senior Lecturer in Organisational Behaviour at the University of Glasgow Business School, Centre for Technical and Organisational Change. He has published four books and a number of articles based on his research in the areas of work design, information technology, and the management of change.

Dr Patrick Dawson is Lecturer in Organisational Behaviour in the Department of Business Studies at Edinburgh University. His main interests comprise new technology and supervision, the development of expert systems for non-experts, new patterns for flexible work.

Nicholas Kinnie teaches industrial relations and personnel management at the School of Management, University of Bath. His main interests in the information technology field involve the study of the managerial implications of new techniques for monitoring and controlling employee activity at work.

Douglas K. Macbeth is Lecturer in Management Studies at the Glasgow Business School, University of Glasgow. His main interests include applications of information technology in manufacturing planning and strategy. Currently researching buyer/supplier relationships in advanced manufacturing supported by the ACME directorate of SERC and local industry.

James McCalman is Lecturer in Management Studies at the University of Glasgow Business School, Centre of Technical and Organisational Change. His research into the linkages between foreign owned and Scottish electronics firms has been published in a number of papers, and the management issues will be explored in a forthcoming book.

Ian McLoughlin is Senior Lecturer in Industrial Relations at the Kingston Business School, Kingston Polytechnic. He has researched extensively on the implications of technological change for work and industrial relations, and is currently involved in a study of innovation in non-union forms.

Christopher J. Martin is Lecturer in Management Information Systems at the Department of Management Studies, University of Loughborough. His research interests include strategic management decision and managerial computing.

Barbara Rawlings is Research Fellow in Organisational Behaviour at Manchester Business School. Current interests include the management of organisational change and the introduction of computerised information systems to the National Health Service.

Howard Rose is Research Fellow in the New Technology Research Group at the University of Southampton. He has been involved in research studies of the introduction of new telecommunications technology. He is currently researching aspects of organisational change in relation to information technology and data processing.

Riitta Smeds is a Lecturer in Industrial Management at Helsinki University of Technology, Finland. Her research concerns the computerisation process of industrial organisations, and the impact of information systems on strategy and structure.

Arjen Wassenaar is a Senior Lecturer in Information Management at Twente University, Denmark, and is involved in a research project about information planning behaviour in the profit and non-profit sector.

Preface

This volume examines the challenge to management which is posed by ever more sophisticated applications of information technology. It reports on cases of actual practice, and seeks to draw lessons from these experiences which will be of practical value to managers and their advisers.

The book had its origin in a workshop held in September 1986 at the European Institute for Advanced Studies in Management, Brussels. This attracted 18 papers and the quality of the papers was such that we felt it worthwhile to make a careful selection of them more widely available. Nine of the conference papers have been selected for inclusion, one specially written paper has been added, and the editors have written an opening and a concluding chapter. So although the book is based on a conference, it is not merely a reprint of the conference proceedings.

We expect the book will appeal particularly to those whose job is to advise and support line managers in the introduction of information technology projects. These may be either internal or external consultants, perhaps with a computing or systems background, or they may be people from a line function who have the job of implementing a major technical change successfully. The book will also be a useful source of ideas, experience and examples to teachers in both further and higher education, and in business schools and management colleges.

Our thanks are due to the contributors to this volume, who co-operated so willingly in meeting the timetable we established. We are especially grateful to Nan Gray, our secretary. She has maintained an efficient and cheerful link with the many contributors, both during the preparations for the conference, and in the production of this book.

David Boddy, James McCalman, David Buchanan
Glasgow Business School

1

The New Management Challenge: Information Systems for Improved Performance

David Boddy and David Buchanan

Developments in information technology, and in the way it is applied, are raising new challenges for managers. Although computers have been part of the business world for almost 40 years, their effect on most organisations has been less than revolutionary. As King (1986) has argued, 'the "nuts and bolts" of many businesses would quickly halt if computers were to stop functioning' (p. 34). But in most instances, 'the computer system and the information that it processes do not serve as a resource that is integral and critical to business success' (p. 34).

That is changing. Continuing technical developments allow radical new links between information technology and the overall strategic direction of an organisation. These possibilities have been shown by, for example, Matteis (1979), Buchanan (1983), Benjamin *et al.* (1984), Rockart and Scott Morton (1984), and Porter and Miller (1985), all of whom show how technology has been used to enhance strategic positions.

It is also clear, however, that the link is not automatic. The real challenge to managers is to take the actions that will turn technical possibilities into business success. Earl (1986), for example, refers to technical developments providing business with 'new strategic *options*' (emphasis added). The management challenge is to perceive those options and to implement them in a way that demonstrably improves business performance.

The chapters in this volume illustrate how this challenge is being met. The contributions are based on direct studies of information technology being introduced into organisations. Taken togethei, they are a source of fact and experience about three aspects of the new management challenge, namely:

1. Monitoring and controlling performance.
2. Establishing direction and purpose.
3. Changing organisation structures.

We expect that this text will be most useful to readers who work with managers in planning and implementing technical and organisational change. Some may have responsibility for information technology projects, but may not be computing specialists. Others may be management services or systems specialists responsible for project management, or for providing advice to functional management. We hope that this book will be a useful source of ideas and stimulus for both these groups of 'promotors' and 'internal consultants' concerned with the effective application of information technology.

Another group of readers will be those conducting research into the management and human aspects of computers and information technology. For them it provides a sample of recent experience, and a review of some current issues, which they can take into account in formulating and interpreting their own research. Similarly, and finally, the book will be useful to those teaching the growing number of courses in further and higher education which include consideration of the management and social aspects of technology. It will highlight some of the issues which merit consideration in such courses, and provide teachers with a source of real examples, cases, and illustrations.

The chapters which follow are based on experience with a range of applications of computing and information technologies. Some of the applications represented in the chapters by Kinnie and Arthurs, Smeds, and Rose can best be described as technical or administrative 'tools'. That is, they represent the use of computers on specific, independent tasks, in a way that raises few if any management issues. For example, they include the use of simple computerised time recorders, 'free standing' computer-aided design, or the use of a mainframe computer to process client records at an insurance company. A much bigger group of cases concerns various forms of integrated management information systems. The cases presented by Buchanan and McCalman, Dawson and McLoughlin, Rawlings and Martin all fall into this category.

The sectors covered are as diverse as the technologies. The cases are drawn from service industry as diverse as hotels, health, railway operations and insurance, as well as from organisations turning out a wide range of manufactured products.

DEVELOPMENTS IN TECHNOLOGY

Rapid and apparently turbulent developments of information technology have led to five types of application. Each is relatively easy to distinguish from the others, and each raises new issues for management and their organisations. Typically, later types of application have tended to augment, rather than replace, the others.

Administrative tools

This refers to the use of computers to perform relatively routine data-processing activities in a prescribed manner. This originally depended on large, 'stand-alone', mainframe computers, processing large volumes of data in batches. More recently mini and micro computers have dramatically widened the range of administrative information which can be processed by computer, and widened the types of staff directly involved. For example, financial or personnel data can now be processed by staff using micros in their own departments, rather than having to depend on a central computer department.

Technical tools

Computers have also been applied to the automation of specific, relatively independent, technical and physical processes of organisations. Early applications were principally in process control operations in industries such as chemicals and power supply. Now they are being applied to a much wider range of tasks such as component design, machine operation, typing and energy management.

Integrated information systems

By linking separate sets of administrative data, and processing them in particular ways, the information can be used by managers as they make decisions on current operations. A computer used only as an administrative tool may concentrate on recording and processing, say, cost information for various 'historical' accounting functions, and can thus be of limited value to current decisions. Technical developments now allow much more data to be captured, processed

3

and transmitted to managers, at a speed and at a degree of detail that makes it of considerable value in dealing with current decisions.

Integrated manufacturing systems

Technical developments increasingly make it possible to link together previously independent 'technical tools' (or 'islands of automation') into integrated manufacturing systems. For example design, planning, manufacture and inspection functions can be linked and controlled from a single computer system, rather than being carried out as separate operations.

Convergence

The convergence of computing and telecommunications systems make it possible to link together previously separate information or manufacturing systems into networks. These may be in the same building or in widely separate places. Information from a computer in a distant office can be sent directly to one at, say, head office, giving corporate management an 'up to date' picture of the business. Similarly the ability to send drawings generated on a computer-aided draughting system in one plant to a similar system in another plant makes possible radical changes in manufacturing arrangements.

FEATURES OF CURRENT APPLICATIONS

Technical developments affect managers only as they are embodied in real applications. The challenges managers then face are also influenced by some or all of the following features of information technology projects. They can be labelled:

1. Transaction-based
2. Foreground tasks
3. Systemic character
4. Open-ended benefits
5. Open-ended costs

A distinctive feature of many current applications is that they can capture data at the source of the original transaction or operation.

4

In banks, hotels, restaurants and garages, for example, the initial transaction with the customer is often keyed directly into a terminal as it takes place. In factories analyses of machine utilisation and performance can be captured directly from software built into the machine's operating programs.

Such information is immediately available for analysis in a way that was not practicable when the primary record of a transaction (say, a customer order, or a service or report) was on paper and needed to be separately keyed into the computer. Faster processing speeds make it possible for that primary data to be analysed immediately and in much greater detail than was possible.

Another current feature is the addition of 'foreground' tasks to the traditional 'background' ones. As long as computers were being used as administrative or technical tools, on essentially 'background' tasks, few managers needed to take much interest. The payroll or accounting systems were important, but customers were probably unaware that computers were being used, and the business could continue even if the system was down.

That is no longer the case. The range of applications has now become so wide that the quality of product and service received by the customer often depends directly on the quality of the computer system used by staff. Though often not apparent to the customer, the provision of many financial, travel and hotel services have depended heavily on computers for years. This dependence is now reaching other sectors of the economy. It is graphically illustrated by this comment from the computer manager at a large hospital, where integrated computer systems were being applied to a very wide range of live administrative processes:

> Something I am very keen on now is to get over to senior managers the message of what happens when you introduce office automation. In applying a function like payroll, if it collapses the data processing expert will put it together somehow. If an office automation system goes down, and you have applied it to the whole administrative fabric, the whole administrative fabric goes down. That is very critical. Imagine something like what happened here last week (a terrorist bomb explosion which caused many casualties); there are hundreds of procedures that immediately have to happen at three o'clock in the morning and the whole administrative end has to be dealt with with total efficiency. If that is the moment your office automation system goes down . . . (from Boddy and Buchanan, 1986, p. 73).

Similarly in manufacturing, many design and production operations are now computer-aided or controlled. As dependency increases, so does management interest in the quality of the computer resource: they are becoming a key resource to all managers, not just those in particular functional areas.

Information technology applications frequently have a systemic character, in the sense that their influence is felt beyond the department or function in which they are installed. The introduction of computer numerically-controlled machine tools, for example, puts new demands on managers in the machining area directly affected — and also on managers responsible for planning, tooling and maintenance. Beyond that they raise issues such as the appropriate way to allocate and measure costs, or the most suitable kinds of payment systems, which involve even wider departmental interests (Ingersoll Engineers, 1982; Department of Trade and Industry, 1985). As office systems are introduced, managers become increasingly conscious of issues of compatibility and integration. They realise that whatever gains they can achieve in their own departments, even more may be gained if their systems can be linked to, say, a database in another department.

A feature of computer projects is often the open-ended nature of the potential benefits. The novelty of many applications, and uncertainty about how they will perform in practice, means that people are often unclear about the benefits expected and obtained.

While it is quite common to hear managers express disappointment that the new system has not lived up to expectations, it is equally common to hear them speak of unexpected benefits. Skilled and committed staff are often able to find new ways of using equipment, to do tasks or produce benefits which had not been expected at the time of the original investment.

Costs too have a habit of being open-ended. While the basic cost of the initial equipment can be established accurately, it is common for managers to observe that the system in its 'final' state ended up costing a great deal more than originally envisaged. Examples of the sources of these extra costs include unforeseen initial costs for things such as building alterations, cables and better peripheral equipment, the cost of maintenance and system support and upgrading facilities, or capacity to cope with new or unexpected demands. In addition, there are the less easily identified, but still incurred, costs of project management, training, and general disruption while major new systems are brought in.

The argument of this chapter is then that the new challenges

6

Figure 1.1: The new management challenge

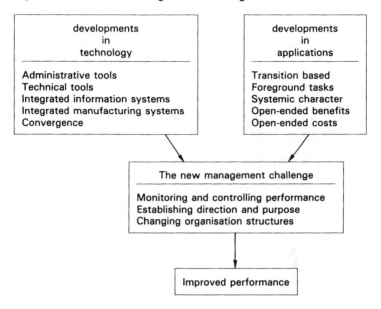

facing managers arise not only from technical developments but also from how the new systems are applied. The more an application is characterised by the five features outlined in this section, the greater the management challenge is likely to be. Three aspects of that challenge will be considered.

1. Monitoring and controlling performance.
2. Establishing direction and purpose.
3. Changing organisation structures.

Each will be introduced briefly in the remainder of this chapter, and then examined further in those which follow. Figure 1.1 summarises the discussion.

MONITORING AND CONTROLLING PERFORMANCE

A key management role is that of monitoring and controlling performance in the area of the organisation for which they are responsible. The ability of computer systems to process large volumes of data has long been used to provide managers with information about performance in their departments or sections. Technical limitations meant that such information, while useful, was slow to arrive and dealt with broad rather than narrow areas of activity. Since the information was often a byproduct of accounting processes, many functions continued to assess their operating performance without the benefit of computer systems.

Technical developments are now making available to managers much more detailed, accurate and timely information on current performance than would have been thought possible only a few years ago. The combination of terminals directly linked to current operations, improved computing power to conduct final analyses, telecommunication links, and desk-top computers can provide managers with much more detailed information on performance in their area. In Chapter 2 David Buchanan and James McCalman illustrate this clearly; the various computer-aided information systems installed in the hotel which they studied provided managers with comprehensive and up-to-date information on all aspects of the hotel's business.

This gave managers a much clearer picture of performance in each section of the hotel, and moreover it was a picture which could be seen by all managers on a consistent basis. This could have direct effects on decisions about pricing and promotional activities, for example. At the same time, it presented managers with new challenges — especially that of coping with greater visibility of their own performance.

In that case, information for monitoring performance reached managers in the conventional form of computer printouts. In Chapter 3, Christopher Martin describes his study of more recent technology for doing the same thing — desk-top systems allowing senior managers direct access to computing. He studied how senior managers used this equipment, and in particular their motives both for initial adoption or rejection, *and* for deciding whether or not to continue to use them. The main reason for managers rejecting such computer systems (even after they had spent a lot of time learning how to use it) was that the information provided was not very useful to the senior managers concerned: 'computer information just could not compete with the information sources which the managers had developed from their existing personal networks' (p. 36).

One of his conclusions, then, is that before there is any significant extension of the use of such systems by managers in their performance monitoring role, a great deal of work is needed by system designers to provide them with the information they need. That in turn implies a challenge to managers, to be able to specify precisely what is at present considered only intuitively — namely the kind of information they really need to monitor and control their area.

A more fundamental challenge on the issue of how to monitor and control performance is posed in Chapter 4, by Douglas Macbeth. He shows that the mere availability of 'high tech' solutions to the information needed for manufacturing does not mean that managers have to choose this route. He argues that an equally viable route is the 'low tech' approach, in which relevant information is localised at the point where it is to be used directly by those responsible for operations: 'If those higher up want to know what is happening, they go down the shop floor and see what the charts say' (p. 46).

This view is of critical significance, showing that though the developments we are discussing pose challenges for managers, those challenges embody choices. Managers can choose whether or not to make use of the technical facilities available. An example of this choice being deliberately exercised was quoted in Boddy and Buchanan (1987), which includes an account of a decision at a large multi-national manufacturing and trading organisation which was planning to install an office automation system at head office. It would have been technically possible to provide direct links to each of its subsidiaries around the world, to provide head office with quicker and more detailed information on local performance, than was available with current methods. This option was rejected by the board, on the grounds that it would conflict with the organisation's policy of decentralised management. As one of the directors explained:

We do not see new technology as a means of getting more control. We do not want to second guess the guy who's there. We don't want them to feel 'well I can leave that, because somebody else is taking the decision.' We often find it quite difficult to explain to suppliers that we *don't* want a real time system with daily sales, cash balances, working capital, management accounts, etc. Our philosophy is that we want people to manage. So we still only really want monthly sales, monthly borrowings, and quarterly management accounts. Anything more than that, and they need lots of bureaucrats; and everyone would be examining their own navels instead of looking at the market place.

9

These examples show that choices exist in how to monitor performance and that the challenge to managers is how to exercise that
choice. The choices made affect managers' experience of work
following the introduction of new technology, and will then affect
overall business performance.

The choices made will also affect the distribution of power within
the organisation. Greater knowledge by managers of their subordinates' performance gives the former an advantage: they can
check performance more precisely and there is less scope for
problems remaining dormant lower down the organisation. This was
forcibly expressed to us by a senior manager in an unpublished study
of a large public utility, which had installed a computerised system
to help manage its service operations. As he explained:

> The management information is good, it is hard information.
> Previously you would go round and ask a depot manager how it
> was going — and a lot of subjective comments came out. Now
> you get a printout which shows what is happening — how many
> calls are beyond the time limit, what the forward workload is,
> etc. It sounds hard, but you can actually pin people down now:
> which is what it is about, holding people accountable.

So while the senior manager in this case felt more confident by
having more information, the depot managers were under greater
pressure, especially those who were having difficulty meeting
performance targets. This would very probably have affected their
attitudes to the system, and their behaviour in relation to it. Other
studies of new information systems which have drawn attention to
their effects on the distribution of power include those by Bjorn-
Andersen and Pedersen (1980) and Markus (1983).

ESTABLISHING DIRECTION AND PURPOSE

Whatever the technical characteristics of a new application may be,
it is management which establishes what kind of contribution it will
make to the business. In some cases, the emphasis has clearly been
on using the technology to improve operating performance in the
production and delivery of current goods and services. The benefits
sought have been those which could be measured, and where quantifiable improvements over current practice could be confidently
expected. Thus new technology is used if it promises to reduce

labour costs, save energy, overcome bottlenecks in production, reduce scrap and so on. In the same vein, computer technology has often been seen as a way of increasing the amount of control which can be exercised over operations, by allowing procedures to be specified more precisely, to reduce dependence on scarce skilled labour, or to ensure a more even and regular pace of work.

Elsewhere, the emphasis on the benefits to be obtained has been different. Technology has been introduced to secure less tangible benefits, such as improving the quality and timeliness of information available to managers, with the intention of enabling more confident decisions to be made. In other cases technical changes have been used to offer new or significantly enhanced products or services, and thus radically shift the position of the organisation in the eyes of its customers or clients.

We have distinguished these two approaches as having either an 'operating' or a 'strategic' emphasis. Which approach is taken is of vital significance to the way the capabilities of IT are used in the organisation, but is, by and large, independent of the technology. The key factor is senior managers' awareness of the scope for strategic uses of emerging technology, *and* its willingness to embark on this much more difficult approach.

The problems of linking information technology to the 'primary business function' is examined by Arjen Wassenaar in Chapter 5. Based on a study of the process by which an engineering company tried to use information technology to reorient the business, he found that it presented managers with new and unexpected challenges. In trying to relate future information systems to future business needs, it 'was very difficult for managers to get a global, but consistent picture of new possible work structures and information structures' (p. 53). He also draws attention to the different cognitive skills required of managers if the more creative possibilities of the technologies are to be realised. 'Managers preferred to think in authority lines and vertical information flows' (p. 54), whereas the strategic uses of the technology involved them in relating information across functional lines.

Learning difficulties of a similar sort are examined by Barbara Rawlings in Chapter 6. She observed the introduction of a major system to computerise personnel and patient records in a district health authority. Both were part of wider, national systems, and the latter in particular is a system of strategic significance to the future shape of health care management. She found a wide knowledge gap between the managers responsible for giving direction and purpose

11

to the organisation, and the computer experts giving advice on the computerisation projects. Like Wassenaar, she implies that if managers are to use the strategic possibilities of new technology, they need a much greater degree of technical awareness, in order to be able to relate successfully to the experts.

CHANGING ORGANISATION STRUCTURE

The third challenge to management is to establish a structure for their organisation which enables the technology to improve performance. Existing boundaries between departments or functions, how jobs are organised within departments, and the balance between centralisation and decentralisation have often been challenged as new information technologies have entered an organisation.

New functions often need to be performed — such as preparing programs for computerised manufacturing operations, plant monitoring and controlling activities, or the provision of support services to new computer services. Consideration needs to be given to the organisation of some existing functions whose role can be radically affected by computer developments of the kind discussed, such as maintenance, office services and production planning. Finally, the spread of microcomputers to a host of new users, often in the 'foreground' line of activities of the business, raise major questions about the functions and reporting responsibilities of the whole computer operation in the organisation.

In Chapter 7, Riitta Smeds describes the evolution of computerisation in a single company from 1974 to the present time. She traces the way computing was organised at different times in that period, and shows how this matched the overall innovative nature of the enterprise. This had on the one hand avoided some of the inertia of tightly controlled systems, but had led to some proliferation of incompatible systems in different parts of the organisation.

This theme, of how to organise computer services, is continued by Howard Rose in Chapter 8, pointing out that the debate on centralised or decentralised computing structures is at least 30 years old. It has been given new issues to consider by the proliferation of microcomputing, the convergence of computing and telecommunications, and the growing position of information technology in the foreground of many organisations. After reviewing six cases, he concludes that there were no technical reasons to favour one form rather than another, and that the crucial issue was the way in which:

'expertise is provided to support that provision of facilities and the system of control that is adopted to regulate it' (p. 98).

A further issue is the way in which the vertical structure of the organisation has been affected by computerisation. This area of management choice was alluded to in our earlier discussion on control, and is further discussed in Chapter 9 by Patrick Dawson and Ian McLoughlin. They show clearly that the introduction of British Rail's system for managing the movement of freight wagons:

> obviated the need for a hierarchical reporting structure. Information about operating conditions and performance at remote locations was now immediately available to Headquarters Management . . . and access to the data was also available at local level (p. 106).

Responsibility for area freight operations had been delegated to local level and this 'in theory made the intermediate level of the old reporting structure redundant' (p. 106). However, this opportunity of structural change was not taken despite the fact that 'the persistence of some elements of the old supervisory system was seen by many as a "barrier" to the full exploitation of the new technological capabilities' (p. 107).

Structural decisions, in the form of the role of supervisors, are also examined by Nicholas Kinnie and Alan Arthurs in Chapter 10. Based on studies of the use of electronic time-recording devices, their conclusion is that:

> supervisors' jobs change in different ways; in some cases their authority is strengthened, while in others it is weakened. These variations are traced back to the strategic decisions managers make in the choice, implementation and operation of the technology employed (p. 120).

In other words they, with the other writers, draw attention to the scope for choice in establishing structure as one of the key challenges to management.

The nature of the new challenge to management should now be clear. It is that in order to exploit fully the technical capabilities of information technology, clear sighted and consistent action is required in three areas. Decisions need to be made about how the functions of monitoring and controlling performance, establishing direction and purpose, and changing organisation structures are to

13

be exercised. Emerging new technologies have challenged existing arrangements in each of these areas.

The following checklists may serve as a guide to the issues which need to be worked on by managers wanting to respond effectively to this challenge.

Monitoring and controlling performance

1. Conduct a systematic review with department managers *and* their staff of the information they really need to do their job.
2. Check that staff have the technical skills to deal confidently with the more detailed and more timely information they can now be given.
3. Ask how they will cope with the extra pressure and stress caused by more visible performance measures.
4. Consider deliberately how far you want to make use of 'high-tech' possibilities, and whether a 'low-tech' solution may be more effective.

Giving direction and purpose

1. Develop adequate technical awareness among senior and middle managers.
2. Develop adequate business and organisational awareness among information technology staff.
3. Ensure that technical choices take account of the strategic direction of the organisation.
4. Establish regular mechanisms to ensure that planning of business processes explicitly includes reviews of technical possibilities.
5. Create project planning teams drawn from a range of relevant functions, and support them in working and thinking across boundaries.

Changing organisation structures

1. Ensure that relevant organisation changes are considered as technical changes are planned.
2. Review the arrangements for managing your computer resources,

including the balance between central and local provision of facilities, and the means for controlling such facilities.

3. Decide whether other support functions should also be reorganised in the light of changing technology.
4. Consider the right balance between central and local decision-making, in the light of technical *and* and market changes.
5. Review how supervisors are being affected by the introduction of information technology, and consider whether the emerging pattern is appropriate.

These checklists serve both to summarise the key points in the chapters which follow, and can be used as a guide to the issues which need to be considered in meeting the new management challenge.

REFERENCES

Benjamin, R.I., Rockart, J.F., Scott Morton, M.S. and Wyman, J.H. (1984) 'Information Technology: A Strategic Opportunity', *Sloan Management Review*, Spring, pp. 3–10

Bjorn-Andersen, N. and Pedersen, P. (1980) 'Computer-facilitated changes in the management power structure', *Accounting Organizations and Society*, 5, pp. 203–16

Boddy, D. and Buchanan, D.A. (1986) *Managing New Technology*, Blackwell, Oxford

—— (1987) *The Technical Change Audit*, 4, The people module, 71, Manpower Services Commission, Sheffield

Buchanan D.A. (1983) 'Using the new technology: management objectives and organizational choices', *European Management Journal*, Winter, pp. 70–9

Department of Trade and Industry (1985) *The DTI Pilots: Evaluation Results*, Department of Trade and Industry Information Technology Division, London

Earl, M. (1986) 'Formulating Information Technology Strategies', in Piercy, N. (ed.), *Management Information Systems: The Technology Challenge*, Croom Helm, London

Ingersoll Engineers (1982) *The FMS Report*, IFS Publications, Bedford

King, W.R. (1986) 'Developing Strategic Business Advantage from Informational Technology', in Piercy, N. (ed.), *Management Information Systems: The Technology Challenge*, Croom Helm, London

Markus, M. Lynne (1983) 'Power politics and MIS implementation', Communications of the ACM, 26 June, pp. 430–4

Matteis, R.J. (1979) 'The New Back Office focuses on customer service', *Harvard Business Review*, 57, March-April, pp. 146–59

Porter, M.E. and Miller, V.E. (1985), 'How information gives you competitive advantage', *Harvard Business Review*, 63, July-August, pp. 149–60

Rockart, J.F. and Scott Morton, M.S. (1984) 'Implications of changes in Information Technology for corporate strategy', *Interfaces*, 14, 1, pp. 84–95

2

Confidence, Visibility and Performance: the Effects of Shared Information in Computer-aided Hotel Management

David Buchanan and James McCalman

INTRODUCTION

This chapter considers how management functions and skills are evolving with the use of computer-based management information systems. Speculation in this area dates from the 1950s, but the kinds of systems now available are different from those in use 30 years ago.

There is not much contemporary commentary on the implications of computing technologies and information systems for management activity. Boddy and Buchanan (1986) summarise recent experience and literature in this area, distinguishing between applications of information systems which managers use themselves, and the secondary effects on management structures where subordinate groups are using computerised equipment.

The literature on work and skills deals primarily with shop and office floor jobs and the role of supervision. The literature on management information systems deals primarily with system design and implementation, and makes little comment on how management roles and responsibilities may be affected in specific organisational contexts.

This chapter presents the results of a study of hotel computing systems which produced management information that was inaccessible using manual routines. The findings are derived from one service sector organisation and their generalisability is therefore limited. But this field has been prone to overstatement and trends may be more reliably identified through idiographic and comparative studies (Bjorn-Andersen and Pedersen, 1980; Barley, 1986).

The findings show that management is affected in three ways by developments in information systems. Confidence in decision-making is increased, performance becomes more 'visible', and managers are pressured for rapid responses to events. The chapter concludes that managers require three key capabilities, concerning knowledge of how computer-based information systems function, ability clearly to specify information needs, and judgement in using new information.

A further conclusion from this study concerns the evolving relationship in which computerised information systems and management development are locked. Managers who have little experience of these systems make demands for, and use, information in ways different from those who have significant understanding. Systems development must therefore respond to the developing knowledge and demands of managers who use them.

Hotel managers in Britain currently have a weak understanding of the problems and opportunities of computing technologies; systems designers have a poor understanding of the information needs of managers (Whitaker, 1984). The technology of computing is still evolving and the range of suppliers and (incompatible) hardware is bewildering. But as the 'new' technologies become 'embedded' in management activity, as systems designers develop their understanding of management needs, and as international standards make systems more compatible, the position reported here will change.

The study

Data were collected in 1985 and 1986 through company documents, non-participant observation of the night audit team and reception work, interviews with 17 members of staff, and an interview transcript feedback process. All but one of those interviewed held managerial positions. Most (13) had been with the hotel since it opened in 1982. Most (14) had no prior experience with computers. The three with computer experience held key management positions. The hotel industry has not been at the forefront of computer use and only larger units have long experience. The systems in this hotel were typical of those in business hotels of comparable size. Gamble (1984, p. 211) describes the range of systems currently available to hotel management.

The property

The Holiday Inn, Glasgow, was one of three in Scotland owned by Commonwealth Holiday Inns of Canada. It had 296 rooms, ten meeting rooms, 6 suites, three restaurants, two bars, and banqueting and conference facilities. The kitchen served 1,200 meals a day. The hotel also had a leisure club, and was the company's 'revenue flagship' in Britain. The hotel employed 250 people with 14 heads of department reporting to a General Manager. The Hotel Accountant was also the Systems Manager, responsible for their effective use. The hotel's business, by room nights, came 65 per cent from the 'business' market, 20 per cent conference and leisure, and 15 per cent from air crews.

The 'business' element generated about 80 per cent of room revenue as half of these guests paid the full rate. Discounts for repeat business were usually 12 to 15 per cent, but could go up to 45 per cent. Discounts for regular tours and airline crews could rise to 65 per cent. Other city properties, particularly in London, operated in the words of one manager as 'bed factories'.

In the Glasgow property, about 60 per cent of revenue and 75 per cent of profit came from room sales. The hotel had a large beverage turnover compared with other Holiday Inns in Britain.

Whitaker (1984, p. 29) argues that 'the velocity of trade and competition for business has increased so much in this sector that computerization is now a virtual necessity in hotels with over 200 rooms'. Gamble (1984, p. 211) identifies the conditions behind this necessity. Reservations are made hours in advance, written confirmation is rare, guests rarely pay deposits, credit is extended on trust, there is a high proportion of 'no shows', with few formal cancellations, the average length of stay is short, stays are frequently curtailed or extended at short notice, and accounts charged to companies are paid slowly. Computing systems have thus been applied to help management to deal with these uncertainties and complexities. But as Gamble (1984) also points out, the hotel customer is still a 'guest' who returns to a hotel because of the quality of personal service it offers. As the General Manager in the Holiday Inn, Glasgow, argued:

> The critical thing for us is that having computers doesn't run the hotel. You can imagine on a busy checkout where you have got 160 businessmen and the computer goes down at the front desk. There is no point blaming the computer. Social skills are needed to cope with that and to combat anything that gives an indication

19

it's computerised. Frankly guests do not want that. All they are interested in is getting the service.

The technology

The property used ten computer systems in 1985:

Micos: for front desk operations and hotel accounts.
Remanco: for customer orders and bills in the restaurants and bars.
Telectron: which monitored use of the private 'Minibars' in each room.
Innfax: free and automatic in-house teletext service.
Holidex: worldwide computerised Holiday Inns reservations system.
Transtel: telephone call logging system.
Bytex: monitoring charges for use of the television film service.
Uniqey: a computerised system of reprogrammable door locks.
Black Boxes: two microcomputers for accounting, cost control, market analysis, personnel records and payroll and word processing.
Energy Remote Control and Optimisation System: a programmable controller for heating and air conditioning equipment.

The two most expensive systems were Micos (at around £80,000) and Remanco (about £16,000). These systems were bought from different suppliers, and were incompatible and functioned independently. Management planned to link some of them, to overcome the need to rekey output from one system into another for further processing, but the technical difficulties had not been resolved at the time of this study. These applications had two notable features. First, they represented an 'invasion ratio' of about 1 to 20; there was one computer system in the property for every 23 full-time employees. Second, despite their pervasive use throughout the hotel, they were operated in a way that made them as unobtrusive to guests as possible.

MANAGEMENT INFORMATION SYSTEMS

The Micos system ran a 'night audit package' which produced a fat pile of printout which included analyses of the hotel's business, including 'no shows', 'travel agents listing', 'checkouts for the day', 'hotel status summary', 'room rate and letting analysis', 'transactions audit list', 'front office trial balance', and 'city ledger transactions list'. Micos then printed statements for the city ledger accounts, and went into a procedure for updating and archiving files. The system then printed a 'room status' analysis showing expected check ins and checkouts for the next day, and listed rooms which were out of order. Then a booking forecast for the next month was printed, based on reservations, and a full guest list showing room numbers and names was produced. The last printout was a folio account for each guest, which could take an hour and was not always run although it was a valuable reference for receptionists. Two copies of all these reports were printed, one for head office and one for the accounts office.

A senior manager explained the implications of this information:

I think that interpreting profit and loss has been very much improved. It has meant that I have been able to involve many more people in the hotel because they all have the same information and they all have it very quickly. You have a printout which is built up from a daily to a monthly basis into a profit and loss for the month for every section of the hotel. All the heads of departments have got the same information and it is easier to get everyone to interpret it the same way.

So I think that it is speed of information and a quick and clear interpretation of that information. And you have to use that. There is no point in having that unless you can use it. Everybody is aware, they can see things happen, they can see trends, and indeed you can develop from that into your sales and marketing strategy for the following three months. We have a market sector analysis, a breakdown of all our sectors every month of where our types of business are on the accommodation side. And all that information is so useful in ringing alarm bells, or spotting potential opportunities. The sales manager sees something, I see it, and everyone is thinking along the same lines. Personally, that is the biggest benefit to me.

Reservations forecasts enabled management to identify peaks and troughs in the business, and to decide when to be rate aggressive and when to be soft on rates. The Regional Sales Manager got a monthly market sector analysis from the Black Box microcomputer, based on information lifted (and rekeyed manually) from Micos. This analysed room nights into eight market sectors, and also generated a 12 month analysis. The Daily Report gave the Executive Chef an analysis of all the food that had been sold. This could help to identify trends in appetites, and also meant that purchasing could be more accurate.

The Transtel telephone logging system produced a printout which enabled the Chief Security Manager to redial numbers called by guests who had left the hotel without settling their bills, to trace them and recover the debt. Staff misuse of the telephones was also controlled in this way (such as Spanish waiters who phoned relatives in South America). The Uniqey computer produced a printout recording all keys cut, at what time and by which receptionist. This information could also be useful for security, for example where a guest's room had been burgled and it was necessary to identify keys issued for that room.

The Remanco system gave restaurant managers detailed information on sales of, for example, bottles of wine, dishes served over one shift, covers served that day, sales per area, at breakfast, lunch and dinner, and the average size of a check paid in the cocktail bar or restaurant. As one manager pointed out, that kind of information could always be found by working manually through restaurant checks, but that was rarely done because it took too much time. One of the managers using Micos information explained that forecasts on occupancies, daily, monthly and annual, made advance budgeting easier and more accurate, rather than being based on juggling manual records and guesswork. Occupancy forecasts also meant that staff rotas could be calculated more effectively, knowing the numbers of guests passing through the hotel on any one day, or in a particular week. Micos also generated automatic reports on guests who had broken their credit limit.

The personnel section used the 'Black Box' microcomputer in the accounts section for personnel records. This recorded sign in and out sheets, and produced the spreadsheets for the '14-day report', a fortnightly analysis of payroll costs. The payroll worked on a two-week cycle. For 13 days, daily reports were produced which analysed the hours worked against budget. The budget was derived from a model of the staffing required to cope with the actual occupancy of the hotel; more guests meant more staff were required in some departments. The personnel records system also produced staff birthday and anniversary lists, could produce a full record for each employee on request, and stored an analysis of leavers. The Remanco system had the potential to monitor the sales of waiters and waitresses, partly as a control on individual productivity, but mainly to enable shift staffing to be established more accurately. This information was, however, not extracted as the system had still to be programmed to produce it.

To monitor energy consumption, each main area in the hotel was metered and monthly readings were taken for billing purposes. These readings, in units and costs, were also passed to an outside firm of consultants who were given information about rooms let, covers served in the restaurants, and laundry articles serviced. This information was then translated into a printed analysis of costs per area which covered the kitchen, main hotel and laundry. The Chief Engineer provided the information and received the analysis. In other words the costs were apportioned, approximately, through the property. This helped to identify areas in which costs were increasing disproportionately. One problem here, however, was that the Chief Engineer could not 'decode' the detailed and complex format of the consultants' analysis printout, and was thus not able to use it. He knew that it contained information of value to him, but complained that he did not have time to decipher it.

THE ROLES OF MANAGEMENT

One senior manager explained that:

> What I think these computer systems do is to make us more professional as a management team, and should release more time for us to spend with the guests. I think that managers have become more efficient as individuals and are probably motivated more towards achieving results because they feel happier and more confident with that information. We do not hide anything. All our heads of departments know exactly how our business is doing. We have a profit and loss meeting every month within our own hotel and everyone has to explain their departmental ups and downs. That is another thing that is important today. People are given the job and encouraged to run it as if it was their business. Therefore it is important that the information we give them is accurate and up to date.

23

The effect of these systems on management was thus to increase:

1. *confidence* in decisions;
2. *visibility* through shared performance information;
3. *performance* through rapid responses to problems and opportunities, higher achievement motivation, and through effective teamwork.
4. the time that managers were able to spend with guests.

In addition, the work of the hotel staff was streamlined, for example through the avoidance of mental arithmetic to add up accounts in the bars, restaurants and at the front desk. These systems gave staff more time to spend with guests, improving the quality of service. This emphasised the *social* skills exercised by staff.

The investment in these systems was justified primarily on the grounds of customer service. It was difficult to identify cost savings to justify the investment in conventional accounting terms. These systems had, however, saved the property significant sums of money in some areas. The energy savings had been spectacular, telephone call monitoring had generated revenue that was previously lost, and unpaid accounts could be identified and collected more rapidly. The system also reduced costs through their contribution to hotel security. At all levels, staff attitudes were positive. Despite criticisms, staff wanted the systems improved and did not want to return to traditional manual procedures.

There were a number of significant *residual problems*. Some management reports from the systems (from Micos in particular) had to be 'hand finished'. Some additional programming would have enabled the computer systems to produce the relevant information in the required formats and would have saved staff time. Some reports, such as those available to the Chief Engineer, had complex formats and were not used. The various systems in use were not integrated. This meant that a lot of information had to be rekeyed (from the other systems into Micos) to compile guest accounts. Improved communications between systems would have saved staff time, although the way in which errors could spread from one system to another was a cause for concern. Guests misused the 'minibars', which were unreliable and generated complaints from guests and staff. The computer which controlled the in-house television system was also not 'guest proof' and could be unreliable.

The computer system used in the restaurants (Remanco) had proved to be too slow for the faster cocktail and lounge bar service.

Management had considered improvements to procedures, such as avoiding the double printing of bills, and returning to manual billing, until a better system was installed. Staff were trained to operate the systems, but had been given no systematic *computer* appreciation. This meant that their understanding of some of the systems was weak, and that on occasion they (unwittingly) misused and damaged sensitive equipment. These residual problems had been recognised and the company's plans for the next generation of systems, due in mid-1986, would confront them.

MANAGEMENT DEVELOPMENT AND SYSTEMS DEVELOPMENT

These findings suggest that the management response to new computer-based information systems should concentrate on three key capabilities. First, managers cannot use information effectively without *system knowledge*, concerning the sources and processing of primary data. Second, managers must be able to *specify needs* for information precisely, to avoid outputs that are unintelligible, irrelevant, or that have to be 'hand finished'. Third, *interpretive ability* is required because although computer systems may help to diagnose problems and opportunities, decisions on appropriate action are the responsibility of management. Rapid and precise analyses increase the demand for managerial interpretation and judgement, to define and resolve problems and to exploit opportunities. This also involves shifts in the context of management decisions, from short-term departmental crisis resolution to long-term co-ordinated strategy.

These findings also indicate how systems development might respond to the spread of (management experience. Management in this case were initially not familiar with systems of this kind, which by 1985 affected all aspects of their business, but were fragmented and incompatible with 'gaps' in their capabilities. There was no unified database, data had to be rekeyed, reports were hand finished and some data were not accessible. These systems were assessed as effective, but management were three years up a learning curve on which they had identified the limitations of their equipment and the scope for further development. This learning was being fed into the next round of system requests.

FUTURE TRENDS

Predicting the future impact of computer-aided decision-making on management activity, Herbert Simon wrote in 1960:

> The plain fact is that a great many middle-management decisions that have always been supposed to call for the experienced human judgement of management and professional engineers can now be made at least as well by a computer as by managers . . . The decisions are repetitive and require little of the kinds of flexibility that constitute man's principal comparative advantage over machines (Simon, 1960).

Leavitt and Whisler similarly argued in 1958 that the work experience of many middle managers in the middle 1980s was going to become more programmed, routine and structured, requiring less experience, judgement and creativity, and receiving less status and reward in return (Leavitt and Whisler, 1958). They did on the other hand predict that rapid technical and market changes would require rapid organisational changes (and they claim in their article to coin the term 'information technology').

Those early predictions demonstrate the dangers in technical and organisational forecasting. Simon's analysis of the impact of computers on the management function was based on the distinction between structured and unstructured decisions. He may have underestimated the predominance of ill-structured problems facing management in the volatile markets of the later twentieth century. Leavitt and Whisler based their forecast on the assumption that better information would mean better management decision-making and control. They may have overestimated the extent to which senior management either want or exercise such detailed control of business operations.

Managers have different decision-making preferences (Yaverbaum and Sherr, 1986). These preferences are likely to influence the course of systems development, which in turn will influence decision-making styles. As more managers find themselves working with these systems, the debate on this subject from the early 1980s may need to be reopened. Management experience and preference is still a topic which system suppliers cannot ignore, as some of our studies in other sectors have indicated (McCalman, 1986).

Reviewing the considerable evidence in this field, Keen (1981) argues that managers generally prefer to base decisions on habit, rules of thumb and muddling through, and that formal analysis of quantifiable information, by any means, is a rare and limited input to decision-making. But contemporary computer systems generate information readily and (comparatively) cheaply, which is more difficult for management to ignore and which demonstrates the poverty of decision-making by hunch, intuition or 'gut feeling' alone. Although performance information will always constitute only a partial basis for management decisions, computer systems are likely to ensure that it plays a more significant role in future, at all management levels.

These computer systems were not a formal, integrated management information system of the kind discussed, for example, by Bridgman and Green (1966) or Ahituv and Neumann (1986). They did not automate the hotel's services, a possibility discussed by Gamble (1984). They were not applied to enhance the competitive advantage of the property in the way that Porter and Millar (1985) suggest. These systems did, however, streamline services and supported management decision-making. Managers claimed that better information led to better decisions, but spoke about these benefits in broad, general terms. These management decision tools were being used *at this stage of development* in an opportunistic way.

Gamble (1984) argues that computing applications in hotels have still to develop beyond basic clerical and administrative functions into strategic decision support. With more managers on the learning curve, demanding improved system specifications, improved procedures to suit their needs, and improved output formats, information systems are likely to move in that strategic direction. The systems installed in this case had been developed by management and staff since 1982 and the process of updating them further by replacement began in 1986. The slope of the management learning curve may thus be comparatively steep.

The managers in this case complained that their systems had been designed by people who did not fully understand the business of a hotel. This lack of business knowledge among systems designers has been noted by several commentators, such as Dagwell and Weber (1983) and Robey (1983), who claims that 'too often, systems design is left to technical specialists who appreciate little about organizational design. Also, organizational designers often demonstrate little awareness of technical options'. Gamble (1984) points out that hotel systems were initially designed by electronics companies following traditional manual hotel procedures which had not developed new ways to perform these with computers. The evidence here implies that systems suppliers in future will be subjected to more rigorous and increasingly intense scrutiny than in the past.

Several commentators have argued that the introduction of computer-based management information systems generates organisational conflicts and power struggles that significantly influence the outcomes (Kraemer and Dutton, 1979; Bjorn-Andersen and Pedersen, 1980; Robey, 1983; Lynne Markus, 1983). These issues did not surface overtly in this case, perhaps for the following four reasons. First, the main systems were installed before most of the staff, including management, were hired. Second, although the systems were chosen by central management services personnel, the need for standard systems, and reporting procedures and formats, throughout the company's hotels in Britain was understood and appreciated. Third, the company had begun to decentralise decision-making in 1985 giving more autonomy to local management. Fourth, the developments up to 1985 had given the local accounting function more responsibility and autonomy, and future developments would extend this. Bariff and Galbraith (1978) argue that accounting and computing staffs who design and administer computing technologies can use them to enhance their own power, influence and control over resources in the organisation. This was happening in this case at the local level, with head office encouragement and apparent local agreement.

First-hand experience with information systems should thus convert more managers from passive recipients of systems to aggressive and active participants in the system design and specification process. But developments will be different in settings where managers have limited or no opportunities to gain that experience. Forecasts in this area thus need to consider the current management, organisational and sector context, and past experience in these areas, as well as current and future technological capabilities.

REFERENCES

Ahituv, N. and Neumann, S. (1986) *Principles of Information Systems for Management*, Wm. C. Brown, Iowa

Bariff, M.L. and Galbraith, J.R. (1978) 'Intraorganizational power considerations for designing information systems', *Accounting, Organizations and Society*, 3, no. 1, pp. 15–27

Barley, S.R. (1986) 'Technology as an occasion for structuring: evidence from observations of CT scanners and the social order of radiology departments', *Administrative Science Quarterly*, 5, no. 1, pp. 78–108

Bjorn-Andersen, N. and Pedersen, P.H. (1980) 'Computer facilitated changes in the management power structure', *Accounting, Organizations and Society*, 5, no. 2, pp. 203–16

Boddy, D. and Buchanan, D.A. (1986) *Managing New Technology*, Basil Blackwell, Oxford

Bridgman, P.T. and Green, J.F. (1966) 'Advanced management information systems', *Management Accounting*, 44, pp. 467–74

Dagwell, R. and Weber, R. (1983) 'System designers' user models: a comparative study and methodological critique', *Communications of the ACM*, 26, no. 11 pp. 987–97

Gamble, P.R. (1984) *Small Computers and Hospitality Management*, Hutchinson, London

Keen, P.G.W. (1981) 'Information systems and organizational change', *Communications of the ACM*, 24, no. 1

Kraemer, K.L. and Dutton, W.H. (1979) 'The interests served by technological reform', *Administration and Society*, 11, no. 1, pp. 80–106

Leavitt, H.J. and Whisler, T.L. (1958) 'Management in the 1980s', in Harold J. Leavitt and Louis R. Pondy (eds), *Readings in Managerial Psychology* (1964), University of Chicago Press, Chicago, pp. 578–91 (reprinted from *Harvard Business Review*)

Lynne Markus, M. (1983) 'Power, politics and MIS implementation', *Communications of the ACM*, 26, no. 6, pp. 430–44

McCalman, J. (1986) 'Overhauling a management information problem', University of Glasgow Information Technology Research Group Working Paper, January

Porter, M.E. and Millar, V.E. (1985), 'How information gives you competitive advantage', *Harvard Business Review*, July-August, pp. 149–60

Robey, D. (1983) 'Information systems and organizational change: a comparative case study', *Systems, Objectives, Solutions* 3, p. 153

Simon, H.A. (1960) 'The corporation: will it be managed by machines?', in Harold J. Leavitt and Louis R. Pondy (eds), *Readings in Managerial Psychology*, University of Chicago Press, Chicago, pp. 592–617

Whitaker, M. (1984) 'The impact of information technology on the hotel and catering industry', Brighton Polytechnic Innovation Research Group, Pilot Project Report, p. 29

Yaverbaum, G.J. and Sherr, D.M. (1986) 'Experimental results towards the customization of information systems', *Human Relations*, 39, no. 2, pp. 117–34

3

Senior Managerial Roles in the Context of Direct Computer Use

Christopher Martin

INTRODUCTION

It has long been the goal of management support theorists and practitioners to establish a basis for computer-based support systems which assist managers directly in their work. The seminal work of Scott-Morton (1971) and others first showed the potential for such systems and highlighted the notion of manager and computer working together as an effective decision-making partnership. Since then, substantial reductions in the real cost of micro-based systems and developments in commercial software have encouraged considerable interest. A significant theme in the orientation of the management support movement has been the interest in systems directed towards the needs of top management, and particularly in strategic and policy-related decision-making. There can be little doubt that computer-originated information is utilised indirectly in one way or another by top management, either through the work of staff advisers or more directly by IT specialists who provide 'chauffeured' access (Culnan, 1983). However, the situation as regards top management's own direct computer use, i.e. the interactive 'hands-on' use of personal computers or terminals, is less clear. In order to explore this area, a case study based research effort has been undertaken (Martin, 1986). This chapter discusses some of the findings from this research and attempts to draw inferences about future directions in management support research and practice.

The research effort was directed specifically at top management, and involved interviewing board chairmen and directors in private companies, and their hierarchical equivalents in public organisations. The principal research questions were straightforward: do top managers use computers directly, and if so, for what do they use them? Does their computer use influence strategic decision processes, and if so, how are such processes affected? In view of some conflicting evidence about managerial computer use found in the literature, a significant question was: why is it that some top managers apparently use computers a great deal while the great majority apparently do not?

RESEARCH METHODS

In order to address these questions, a series of semi-structured interviews was conducted with top managers in a range of UK private and public organisations. In all, over 60 executives were interviewed. Table 3.1 shows an analysis of respondents. At this juncture it must be stressed that there are a number of practical and methodological difficulties associated with research at top management levels. The first problem is one of access; top managers are notoriously difficult people to get to see. Pahl and Winkler (1974) note that perhaps 85 per cent of approaches by researchers may be refused, even with personal introductions, and this leads directly to various difficulties regarding both the choice of research method and also the validity and reliability of findings from what may be a small and/or self-selected sample.

Table 3.1: Details of respondent categories

	Private sector	Public sector	Small firms	Misc.	Totals
Pre-adoption		15	10	1	26
Adopted: pre-trial		2		1	3
Rejected: pre-trial	1	4		1	6
Discontinued users	9	1	4		14
Slight users	2	2		1	5
Moderate users	2	2		1	5
Heavy users	2	1	2	3	8
Totals	16	27	16	8	67

In order to overcome these difficulties and to maximise the validity of the results, a strategy was devised whereby once suitable organisational access had been achieved, strenuous attempts were made to see all the top managers in that organisation. In practice, the research effort resulted in better than two-thirds of target respondents interviewed from five large organisations, and these became the primary source of material used in this chapter. A more detailed description of the access and interviewing methodology is contained in Martin (1986). As well as interviewing the top managers themselves, information was gained from systems development and implementation personnel, from the study of internal documents, and from investigating relevant computer systems and associated materials.

Interview questions were directed towards three main areas:

1. Personal factors, including previous computer exposure.
2. Computer systems available to the manager, and the manner in which they were developed.
3. The precise nature of the manager's computer use in relation to his work roles.

The case study data enabled comparisons to be made between managers from different organisations, and perhaps more importantly, between managers from the same organisation. In this way it was possible to compare data from respondents who were using a computer with data from others in the same organisation who had access to the same facilities but who were not using them. In fact, it was these latter comparisons which were particularly important in answering questions about the nature and circumstances of the managers' computer use.

ANALYSIS OF MANAGERIAL BEHAVIOUR

A key finding from the interviews was that many managers had recently undertaken some form of direct computer use. However, a crucial point was that a proportion of them had discontinued their use after a trial period. The question which naturally arises is: why is it that these managers abandoned their systems? Alternatively, why did other managers in similar circumstances continue their systems use? Of course, not all managers in the survey had adopted personal computing at the outset, even though extensive facilities were available to them, whilst some others continued to utilise their systems to a greater or lesser extent. In general, it is useful to view the activities of the managers in terms of a cycle of behaviours, commencing with initial computer adoption followed by a period of attempted direct use with subsequent continuance or discontinuance. All the managers in the sample could usefully be regarded in terms of this general model of behaviour, and could be categorised

Figure 3.1: The computer adoption process

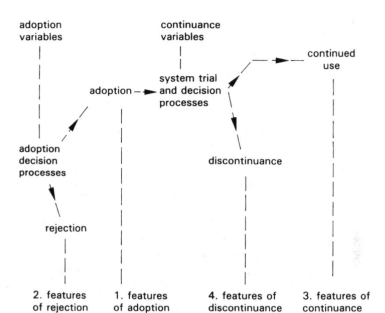

according to their decisions at two key points. In fact some of the managers had already been through two or more of these adoption-discontinuance cycles, and it could be expected that others would do so at least once more in their careers.

A process model which generally describes these behaviours is shown diagramatically in Figure 3.1. The model shows an initial decision process which results either in adoption of a computer system, or in rejection. If the system is adopted, then there is a trial phase followed either by continuing use, or discontinuance. An important feature of the model is that it implies that there are two different sets of variables which come into play at the two key points in the cycle. Usually it is assumed that there are variables which generally influence computer use; here, it is suggested that the set of variables which influences initial adoption is substantially different from the set of variables which influences subsequent continuance.

The key questions about managerial computer use revolve around the circumstances under which some managers reject direct

33

computing when others adopt it, and why some managers continue with their system use when others discontinue. Utilising comparative data derived from the research study, certain features of their circumstances can be associated with the managers' decisions at the two key points in the adoption cycle.

Features of adoption

Managers were influenced by others within the organisation at various levels and rarely was the decision to adopt an individual's lone choice. Although it might be supposed that top-level managers have complete discretion over these choices, in practice they usually described the ways in which they were influenced by others.

Nearly all the managers referred to their leadership roles when describing their computer adoption. In some instances this occurred in the context of a requirement to lead their direct subordinates with respect to computer use; in others because they were in charge of a division with responsibility for the computing resource, and hence there was a need to show appropriate usage leadership to other divisions on behalf of the manager's subordinates. Even where there were no direct functional responsibilities of this kind, senior managers described the requirement for them to reflect positive values with respect to computing, to others both inside and outside the organisation.

Managers had certain expectations with regard to the computer systems which they would receive, in terms of personal informational benefits. These expectations varied, depending partly on the manager's prior experience of direct computing; where the manager had no previous experience the expectations were often unrealistically favourable, leading to subsequent expression of substantial disenchantment and disappointment following system trial.

Features of rejection

In most respects the features of rejection reflected a corollary of the features of adoption. In a few instances, managers had specifically declined to take up direct computing for themselves even though their board colleagues had done so. Either the internal pressures to adopt had been less acute in their particular circumstances, or they had specifically resisted the pressures. With regard to their leadership requirements, either they perceived there to be no requirement for them to display pro-computing values, or, as in one instance, the manager perceived that computer use would reflect negatively on his position.

Features of continuance

A number of managers in the study were presently utilising their computer systems to one degree or another; it was noted that a significant characteristic of their use was the tendency to stick with one particular system or facility, even where a wide range of facilities was available. This was understood to be a response to the need to minimise the personal time and effort costs which were associated with learning how to use new systems.

A significant feature of the continuing use was the direct utilisation of a system within the manager's present work activities. For example, personnel directors used their terminals to access data on individuals from computerised databases; this activity would have been carried out before computerisation using record cards or other means and the automation represented a straightforward replacement of one access mechanism for another. Other top managers who used their systems regularly had all found some way in which their computer use related to current activities. None of the respondents made any significant use of generalised decision support systems, even where these systems were very extensive and sophisticated. In general there was little evidence that any manager's work roles had changed significantly as a result of his computer use. All respondents were asked about the way in which direct computer use had altered their personal work activities, and most of them denied that there had been any significant change.

What was particularly noticeable was that systems use did not appear to confer any particular informational advantage on the user (and some systems were compared unfavourably to alternative access methods). In particular, many of the top managers in the study could command significant human informational resources in terms of staff advisers, financial analysts, and so forth. The direct computer facilities were considered to be poor alternatives to such resources except under special circumstances. In many instances, continuing computer use seemed to be related to the achievement of other goals, particularly as regards the influence of others or the

35

expression of values with respect to the man and his organisation.

Features of discontinuance

All the discontinuing managers described difficulties in terms of time and effort costs associated with learning to use computer systems. It must be emphasised that many of the respondents had made very determined efforts to utilise their systems, and had acquired substantial knowledge about the systems before ceasing to use them. For many respondents, the value of the information to be had from the system seemed to represent a poor reward for the considerable efforts required to access it.

It has been found most useful to consider the computer system as being aimed at addressing various aspects of the manager's informational and decisional roles; it appeared that the systems failed to do this successfully because the systems were incorrectly oriented as regards the particular nature of senior managerial work in respect of these roles. In particular, where the information was aimed, for example, at monitoring or resource allocation roles it often reflected issues which would be of more interest at lower management levels. Apart from the orientation failure, it seemed that this computer information just could not compete with the information sources which the managers had developed from their existing personal networks.

It is a characteristic of senior managers that they acquire and develop superior information sources through skilful manipulation of interpersonal networks (Kotter, 1985). Attempts to create and implement systems which were to compete directly with these sources (even formally based ones) seemed to have been ineffectual. In a similar way, the managers' liaison and dissemination roles were usually not enhanced by computerised messaging systems, partly because the systems did not include important contacts who were part of the manager's interpersonal networks, and partly because they lacked the immediacy of face-to-face contacts or the efficiency (for the managers) of traditional methods.

DISCUSSION

It was possible to analyse the computer systems which had been made available in terms of the managerial roles which the systems were intended to address. A useful representation of the different roles enacted by managers has been developed by Mintzberg (1973), who has identified ten different managerial roles: figurehead, leader, liaison, monitor, disseminator, spokesman, entrepreneur, disturbance handler, resource allocator and negotiator. It is of course necessary to point out that Mintzberg's theory, as it relates to these ten specific roles, is not without its critics; in particular Luthans, Rosencrantz and Hennessey (1985) cite studies which do not show direct empirical support for Mintzberg's categories. However, it can be argued that what is important here is not whether certain specific senior managerial roles are universally prominent or not, but rather that it is recognised that a number of very different roles exist in managerial work, many of which are not directly concerned with 'decision-making' or 'information processing' as these are commonly understood.

Referring to the role structure of Mintzberg, it can be shown that the computer systems in the study were intended to support the manager's decisional and monitoring roles primarily, although in some cases messaging systems were provided which were intended to support liaison and disseminator roles. The other interpersonal roles of figurehead and leader were not intentionally addressed by any of the systems, even though for senior managers such roles might be expected to be especially significant. In practice, the managers considered the consequences of adoption in terms of their own leadership role most carefully, and it seemed that for most of the respondents these considerations were more important to them than any other in their adoption decision.

In the second phase of the adoption cycle, the manager's decision to continue his computer use (or to discontinue it) seemed to be based on a balance between the effort and rewards occasioned by the initial and ongoing effort costs on the one hand, and the informational and behavioural benefits on the other. For many respondents in the study the former far outweighed the latter. The important point is that simply improving the man/machine interface aspects, for example, will not necessarily help matters; if the system information remains incorrectly oriented, or represents bad value for other reasons, then the manager will perceive that his efforts are not sufficiently rewarded and he will discontinue, however 'user friendly' the interface may be. This is illustrated by the fact that many of the managers in the sample had made strenuous (and largely successful) efforts to overcome considerable interface and learning difficulties, but had then discontinued when they found out for themselves the precise nature of the system's real information value in terms of their real roles.

SUMMARY

The two-phase behavioural model of the computer adoption process provides a framework for considering key aspects of the circumstances of computer use by top managers. Where managers had discontinued their computer use, this was associated not only with significant difficulties (and hence personal effort costs) at the man-machine interface, but also with a failure of the systems to provide adequate rewards which would offset those costs. On the one hand the computer systems addressed limited aspects of the manager's role set, and on the other there appeared to be errors of orientation with respect to the top manager's special informational needs and activities.

If these findings are generally applicable — and there appears no reason why this should not be so, at least as regards large organisations — then there may be a considerable opportunity for the development of new systems for top managers. The basis of such new systems would be the development of facilities which directly address those managerial roles which so far have remained largely untouched by current developments in information technology.

REFERENCES

Culnan, M.J. (1983) 'Chauffeured Versus End User Access to Commercial Databases: The Effects of Task and Individual Differences', *MIS Quarterly*, March

Kotter, J.P. (1985) *The General Managers*, Free Press, New York

Luthans, F., Rosencrantz, S.A. and Hennessey, H.W. (1985) 'What Do Successful Managers Really Do? An Observational Study of Managerial Activities', *Journal of Applied Behavioural Science*, 21, 3

Martin, C.J. (1986) *A Behavioural Analysis of the Adoption and Use of Interactive Computer Systems by Senior Managers*, unpublished PhD thesis, University of Durham

Mintzberg, H. (1973) *The Nature of Managerial Work*, Harper & Row, New York

Pahl, R.E. and Winkler, J.T. (1974) 'The Economic Elite: Theory and Practice', in P. Stanworth and A. Giddens (eds), *Elites and Power in British Society*, Cambridge University Press, Cambridge

Scott-Morton, M.S. (1971) *Management Decision Systems*, Graduate School of Business Administration, Harvard University, Boston

4

Manufacturing Information Systems at the Crossroads

Douglas Macbeth

Manufacturing management is at a stage in its evolution where major choices have to be made about the appropriate future direction to be travelled. Information systems provide the means of recognising these choices and provide of themselves different routes to the future.

We have firstly to recognise two kinds of information requirement in manufacturing. The first is information as a tool of strategic management while the second relates to the needs of operational management within the manufacturing function. Within this operational area we are now recognising what can be called a High Tech (HT) and a Low Tech (LT) approach with quite different information technology requirements.

STRATEGIC INFORMATION

The strategic aspects of manufacturing information relate to the nature of a manufacturing system which must be consciously designed to do certain things well.

Like any design process a trade-off situation often applies in that by choosing to do one thing well a perhaps less conscious choice is being made to do something else not quite so well. Wickham Skinner in his seminal article (1969) argued that a lack of top management awareness of these factors leads to the situation of senior management delegating often major facility decisions to lower levels of manufacturing management who select options without an apprecia- tion of the strategic needs of the business. In this way decisions which make sense in the short run come to tie the plant to inappropriate process technologies for the longer term.

The strategic information flow should be in an interactive loop. Information from the market place must be obtained in a form appropriate to manufacturing decision-making. This will not necessarily be the same as that obtained by another function. For example to a salesman an order worth £100 is essentially the same as another order for another £100. To manufacturing, however, this need not be true. Manufacturing must break down the aggregated sales figure into detailed product, component, part lists, each to be fitted into a planning, production and control process which will produce products to actually satisfy the £100 order. In similar fashion a new product design must also be broken down into precise detail for manufacturing purposes. In both cases, however, it is the mix of different product types within the total that will have a major impact on manufacturing's ability to produce. To manufacturing then one order for 100 different items at £1 each does not equate to another order for 100 identical items at £1 each. Thus information flowing into manufacturing must recognise its need for detail.

Manufacturing has, however, a responsibility to communicate in the opposite direction details of the constraints under which it operates. It may not be possible for them to change their output type as quickly as the market ideal might suggest and therefore it might be good business sense to play to existing strengths and support more extended production runs. (In many cases it makes even more sense to develop effective means of making the change.) Similarly previous process investment decisions might make certain new product ideas not so immediately realisable while existing processes may have capability not suitably matched to particular quality standards. Existing production commitments might also mean that a new rush order may just be possible to deliver on time but for this job going through faster than normal usually at least one other will be delayed. The impact of this kind of information on customer satisfaction must also be generated.

Of course what wins orders for a company's products in the market place is not always manufacturing excellence as such but manufacturing must be organised to support what Hill calls the order winning criteria. To properly identify such factors does demand a full and free exchange of information to permit fully informed judgement to enable manufacturing to 'provide better than the company's competitors those criteria which enable the products involved to win orders in the market place' (1985).

This information exchange offers real possibilities for IT support in evaluating impacts of decisions and for modelling possible options. It can also provide a more integrated view of the total business system using common information, the accuracy of which all functions accept.

OPERATIONAL INFORMATION

The above discussion largely relates to information needs which address an outwards look from the company to the customer. There is an overlap to the information needed to run the day-to-day operations of the manufacturing area. Information is needed in each of the following categories: product; materials; process types and machine capabilities, people involved with the whole process and associated financial measures associated with each of these. The manufacturing information needs do not always accord with other information systems employed in the plant. For example normal cost accounting practices can make it difficult to realise exactly what a particular process element costs to utilise. The practice of absorbing overhead and sharing it out over each process, cost centre, product, person employed, etc., can make it more difficult to determine the actual contribution each part makes to the whole. Even traditional approaches to investment appraisal for manufacturing process investment have been criticised as being too severe and short term in focus (Kaplan, 1986; Hill, 1985, pp. 159–200). The operational information requirements revolve around the answers to the following questions.

What do we need to produce? — products, parts, etc., to satisfy the demand on the system.
When are these things needed? — in effect a priority system and an ordering of the sequence of activities.
Where and how will we manufacture these items — which processes must they traverse on their route through the factory — are there single or multiple routes? Is there a cost penalty in duplicate routings? Is there a machine process which controls our effective system output?
What quantity and quality is required for each of the customer orders? Does this impact on answers to previous questions?
Who will do the work in conjunction with the physical process? What skills, discretion, decision making capability and authority should they have?
How will we organise the complexity and control performance

41

against what plan, specified by what criteria of measurement and required performance?

MANUFACTURING INFORMATION SYSTEMS — POSSIBLE SOLUTIONS

The traditional approach was through a policy of stock-holding to satisfy the expected demand (unknown in precise quantity or timing). This approach is built around Economic Order Quantity (EOQ) approaches. Given the assumptions underlying the theory the mathematical precision of an approach which balances the costs of procurement against the costs of holding stock was high and the attempt was made to apply this thinking in manufacturing (as well as purchasing) decision areas. To replace the relatively fixed cost of placing an order another (assumed) fixed cost of set-up time was taken. The development of what was now referred to as Economic Batch Quantities then followed precisely on with the usual result that the most 'economic' length of production run was very long and usually greatly exceeded actual customer requirement at that time. (Note, however, that the mathematical formula shows that as set-up costs tend to zero batch sizes also tend to zero.)

Materials Requirements Planning (MRP) first evolved in recognition that the demand for the components of a given product is dependent on the demand expressed for the product and is absolutely calculable given that starting point. MRP thus works for an agreed manufacturing requirement (agreed between Marketing and Manufacturing as acceptable and achievable) through details of product structures (supplied by Design) through to materials control information about current availability and time to manufacture/purchase the actually required quantities for a given time period. The approach can be expanded into MRP II, Manufacturing Resource Planning in which form the system covers all of the companies' activities (including financial management) in a totally integrated way and approaches what Orlicky terms 'a new way of life in production and inventory management' (1975). This approach is computer intensive with highly formalised information handling procedures.

MRP and EOQ can be criticised as being 'push' systems in that having in some way determined what manufacturing ought to produce this information is 'pushed' into the system in the hope and expectation that the desired products come out the other end as planned. In many cases, however, the plan is in anticipation of actual customer demand and therefore may not actually meet a changed requirement.

Optimised Production Technology (OPT) (Harrison, 1985; and Goldratt and Cox, 1986) is one approach to this problem in that it essentially works on the premise that the objective of the business is to produce output which can immediately be turned into sales income. The planning and control process (and therefore the information need) is geared towards those few processes which constrain the amount of 'throughput' (i.e. product for immediate sale), i.e. the bottleneck operations. Planning is based on maximising utilisation of the bottleneck while everything else is based on supporting or working from the bottleneck. This approach still calls for extensive computer support to handle the detailed scheduling involved to maximise throughput.

The approaches outlined so far accept as given the complexity of producing a variety of products in a complex interconnected network of material and information flow paths. Mass production industries in chemicals, for example, have long taken a different approach with notable economic success.

These lessons have been applied to other high-volume businesses, e.g. motor vehicle manufacture, initially by Toyota of Japan (Ohno and Kumagai, 1980). Their approach called Just-in-Time (JIT) operates on a quite different philosophy — one of constant striving for improvement and gearing production output more closely to customer demand. It also aims to eliminate waste of any kind but especially inventory, for the Japanese recognised that inventory might appear on Western balance sheets as Current Assets but in fact it is a liability. In the UK a recent estimate was some £23bn tied up in inventory costing £5bn per year in capital financing charges alone. Too much inventory in fact creates problems while at the same time hiding others.

JIT is a 'pull' system which works on the basis of a final assembly schedule designed to satisfy the current customer requirement. Once the final assembly stage completes work on a product they 'pull' material from feeding stages. Only then do these stages get the signal to produce more material just in time for the succeeding stage to work with. These signals range from cards, to painted squares on the floor, even to coloured golf balls rolling down a tube (Schonberger, 1982). The essence is that complexity is removed from the process, effort is continuously applied to reducing set-up times to enable fast change-over of product types and to improving quality and breakdown-free plant operation. The system involves all the work people and information is highly visible and not dependent on computerisation at the shop floor. MRP systems can be used for forward planning purposes, however.

MAIN ISSUES AND IMPLICATIONS

Each of these various developments is in addition to major innovations in manufacturing technologies and in IT applications in product design especially. In many cases the IT aspects allow for much greater product variety and a faster rate of change.

In all cases we can see the same issues emerging. The first is that these technologies can exist alone but that the real benefit comes from taking a total systems view. For example a computer-aided design system on its own shows little productivity improvement over traditional methods but put it into an integrated manufacturing system and lead times can reduce substantially through efficient information handling avoiding wasteful transcription processes. Many of them are also integrative of themselves and because of this the strategic impact of success or failure in one area of the system is going to cause impacts on very many other areas.

We thus have one of the major implications of the new information management requirement and that is that the management of the business must have a much more encompassing view of the totality of the business and must also have a vision of a desirable future and an appropriate path towards it. This vision must be translated into a strategic framework within which detailed operational decisions can be made.

The second main issue is that managers in manufacturing have choices to make about how they are going to organise and manage the function. While a hybrid approach targeting particular solutions for particular market requirements might make a lot of sense a choice exists between what can be called the High-Tech and Low-Tech approaches (HT & LT).

The HT approach can be characterised as Complexity/Computerisation/De-skilling while the LT approach can be characterised by Simplification/Visible Controls/Employee Involvement. The HT approach is heading along the technically exciting path towards Computer Integrated Manufacture and the Automated Factory (Bylinsky, 1983), while the other sees such solutions only to be appropriate in very limited circumstances.

It is hard to see this as a pure choice since the market situations currently being addressed by the two approaches are somewhat different although both would claim to be heading in the same direction, to economic batch sizes of 1. At the present time the HT approach is largely aimed at Batch manufacture of a variety of goods while the LT way has most of its major exponents at a higher market volume/reduced variety sector of demand. There is, however, an argument that the total systems benefits of the LT approach are so great that a move into the lower volume/higher variety sector would be similarly successful.

The two approaches have quite fundamentally different approaches to manufacturing information. Each approach is built around certain basic principles almost at opposite ends of a continuum. HT is predicated upon computerised databases and communications in which the sheer formalism of the computer system requires that data accuracy and maintenance are at extremely high levels or failure is guaranteed. Wight (1981), for example, quotes inventory accuracy levels of 98 per cent and Bill of Material (parts list and assembly structure) information in the same range as being prerequisites. This accuracy requirement also makes obligatory formalised data capture from the shop floor to keep information timely. This in itself can create a requirement for computerised shop floor data recording technologies of laser scanners, magnetic code readers, etc.

The levels of automation in the process also argue for new information requirements. De-skilling of the actual productive process creates requirements for new skills in programming and planning manufacturing processes and can provide for fewer technical specialisms as the design computer system begins to encroach into formerly distinct decision areas. Here again choices can be made. Buchanan reports one company choosing to retain human skills at the process machine rather than allow support personnel all of the autonomy (1986).

The essence of the LT approach is indicated in the subtitles of Schonberger's books where simplicity is seen as the initial target of any improvement in manufacturing. Computerisation is seen as an appropriate solution only once more human scale improvements have been exhausted.

Thus the challenge is to create simplicity out of complexity, often by recognising the benefits of Focus (Skinner, 1974) and a strategic decision about what a given (usually smaller) manufacturing unit must be good at. Much information processing and creativity has to be applied at this stage. Toyota have taken over 20 years to produce what we now call their Just-in-Time system. During that time intense production engineering efforts have gone into making the process more predictable. controllable and error free. That process has also extended backwards into the supplier areas to manage them as 'outside factories' or 'partners in progress'.

Because the manufacturing task is much simplified and material flow is uncomplicated, the need is not there for complex data gathering for each stage in the process. In fact the ideal is seen as a black box approach. That is, whatever is produced as output accounts for all inputs and all internal transactions.

The accounting and supplier payment systems work on that total system basis rather than on individual manufacturing or purchase orders or on an individual cost centre control approach.

The operational people are seen as the key resource in the LT approach. Since total quality control is mandatory every person has a personal responsibility not only to get it 'right first time' but also continually to strive for improvement.

This creates a requirement for a different form of manufacturing information. This time it is localised and related to the search for improvement. Visible control by means of statistical process control charts, graphs of improvement patterns, performance indicators against plan, etc., are prominently displayed at the workplace. In state of the art plants this is the only place the information exists. It is not automatically passed up the managerial pyramid. If the managers want to know what is happening on the shop floor they do not interrogate their desk-top computer terminal — they go down on the shop floor and see what the charts say! (Schonberger, 1986)

Such systems are seen as inherently more flexible. The HT approach utilising automated assembly machines, robots, etc., does in theory have a capability to operate more continuously and often unmanned. Currently the requirement to design products in such a fashion that facilitates assembly by robots often produces the interesting result that humans can perform the operations equally successfully (if not so continuously or perhaps inherently so error free). The additional flexibility of the human to change tasks quickly provides opportunities for coping with variety that may exceed that of the HT solution.

Two short examples might illustrate the differences between the two. The HT approach is typified by the manufacturer of flat-pack DIY kitchen furniture whose approach has been highly IT intensive to the point that a customer can telephone an order, have delivery confirmed (following interrogation of the computer system) and have it delivered at the precise hour by the company's own transport. The manufacturing process itself is highly automated and uses little labour. The LT approach is exampled from the seat and trim area of Jaguar cars reported by Stokes (1987). An original system of storage in anticipation of planned demand and issue according to schedule created problems when body assemblies were rejected on the line causing seats and trims to be returned to stores. To solve this problem a girl was placed in the body shop and another in the trim shop. Every time a good body passed the first girl she read its number and trim details, telephoned her colleague who initiated production of the appropriate materials which were easily manufactured and supplied in the four hours that the body took to complete its body shop operation. This simple approach eliminated a week's stockholding and avoided wasted manufacturing effort on trims which could not be used due to reject bodies. Note, however, that in this example a simple piece of automation could eliminate the need for both girls! In effect all that is required is some kind of sensor of model type and a communication link back to trim manufacture. This nicely illustrates the simplify and then automate if appropriate approach taken in the LT approach.

Manufacturing management in these two approaches is quite different in nature, scope and focus. The change from one to the other is not to be lightly undertaken and not for reasons that are any less than totally understood and recognised as appropriate to the business objectives — the difficulties of implementing such changes and the implications for the rest of the system are simply too great.

SUMMARY

Manufacturing industry is at a critical stage in its evolution. Many long held beliefs and practices are being shown not to be universally valid. We need to re-examine all the 'taken for granted' assumptions with which we currently operate and challenge their appropriateness and contribution to future success in increasingly competitive global markets.

In essence we must recognise that manufacturing information is a strategic commodity which must flow around the whole system and be translatable to precise local needs.

Effectiveness of the total system in satisfying the customer is the new critical factor which may be affected by the 'efficiency' of one interdependent functional area having an adverse impact elsewhere in the system.

For this reason managers must have a total systems viewpoint with a vision of a desirable future and of the path(s) which lead there.

That future may encompass a High Tech or a Low Tech solution to the operational design of a manufacturing system. Depending on the choice made there are major differences in the nature, form, substance and location of manufacturing information and critically the roles and task structures of people in the system.

REFERENCES

Buchanan, D.A. (1986) *Canned Cycles and Dancing Tools: Who's Really in Control of Computer Aided Machining*, Working Paper No. 1, University of Glasgow, Department of Management Studies, Glasgow

Bylinsky, G. (1983) 'The Race to the Automated Factory', *Fortune*, 21 February, pp. 52–64

Goldratt, E.M. and Cox, J. (1986) *The Goal*, Creative Output Books, Hounslow

Harrison, M.C. (1985) 'The concepts of Optimized Production Technology (OPT)', *Proceedings 20th European Tech. Conf. BPICS*, pp. 15–28, Bishop's Stortford

Hill, T. (1985) *Manufacturing Strategy*, Macmillan, London

Kaplan, R.S. (1986) 'Must CIM be Justified by Faith Alone?' *Harvard Business Review*, March–April, pp. 87–95

Ohno, T. and Kumagai, T. (1980) 'Toyota Production System', *Proceedings of Int. Conf. on Industrial Systems Engineering and Management in Developing Countries*, Bangkok

Orlicky, J. (1975) *Material Requirements Planning*, McGraw-Hill, New York

Schonberger, R.J. (1982) *Japanese Manufacturing Techniques: Nine Hidden Lessons in Simplicity*, Free Press, New York

——— (1986) *World Class Manufacturing: The Lessons of Simplicity Applied*, Free Press, New York

Skinner, W. (1969) 'Manufacturing — Missing Link in Corporate Strategy', *Harvard Business Review*, May–June, pp. 136–49

——— (1974) 'The Focused Factory', *Harvard Business Review*, May–June, pp. 113–21

Stokes. P. (1987) 'JIT in Application', *Low Inventory Manufacture*, Conference organised by Midlands Operational Research Society at University of Birmingham, March

Wight, O.W. (1981) *MRPII: Unlocking America's Productivity Potential*, OWL Publications, Williston, Vermont

5

Information Management in an Industrial Environment — an Educational Perspective

Arjen Wassenaar

INTRODUCTION

You can't plan tomorrow's management education programmes with today's assumptions. For this reason we will consider the changing context of organisations, the management of these organisations and their use of information technology in the future. The purpose of computer application in organisations is changing. Application opportunities in the sixties and seventies were limited to Management Information Systems for planning, management control and operational control. This conventional perspective on information systems was directed at automating basic processes and satisfying management information needs (Wiseman, 1985). These systems have reached a relatively high degree of maturity and integration and have become relatively standard systems. Our educational programmes are mostly based on this conventional MIS perspective.

In the eighties and nineties the focus of automation will move towards the primary business functions. This so-called strategic perspective (Wiseman, 1985) on information systems will be directed at information technology opportunities in the primary processes of engineering, manufacturing, sales and distribution. These applications will have a direct impact on competitive positions and added value. New information technology will become a tool to drive business operations, which will not only affect the existing patterns of business but will call for new, integrating concepts of management.

The chapter begins by drawing attention to two views about tomorrow's organisations and their environment. Then the implementation of information technology in the business processes of a Dutch engineering construction company is discussed. Finally, a case for new management concepts and their incorporation in effective education programmes is made, based on case study experience.

THE CONTEXT OF DISCONTINUOUS CHANGE

Alvin Toffler (1984, 1985) predicts that new technology will make diversity as cheap as uniformity. Based on computers and numerical control demassified production is possible, with short, even customised production runs. He stresses that demassification is one of the key causes of the information revolution. In distribution he expects more market segmentation, direct mail targeting, special stores, even individualised delivery systems based on home computers and teleshopping. Toffler suggests that in the future mass production and mass distribution will no longer be advanced methods. There will be a lot of do-it-yourself production (self service). The so called invisible producers in the cottage industries will also grow.

These examinations of the future will bring a new worker. He will be more independent, more resourceful, no longer an appendage of the machine. Mind workers have skills and information that amount to a kit of head tools. They own the means of production in a way that unskilled factory workers never could.

Akio Morita, co-founder of Sony, said, 'I can tell a factory worker to show up at 7.00 am sharp and produce, but I can't tell a researcher or engineer to show up at 7.00 and have a creative idea.' Toffler expects these resourceful, innovative, educated, even individualistic workers will invent their own form of organisation: more associational, less homogenising.

Toffler describes a model of the future super-industrial corporation consisting of a slender, semi-permanent framework from which a variety of small, temporary 'modules' are suspended. These move in response to change and can be spun out or rearranged as required by shifts in the outside world.

Handy (1980) states that 'the feeling that trusted ways and known formulas have disappeared in the kick of discontinuous change'. Planning can only cope with continuous change. Discontinuous change needs an alternative approach of controlled experiment to cope with change, and a different type of person (a risk oriented, scientific optimist) to manage it.

Therefore Handy expects these changes will not come from

existing institutions but from new ones that will bypass their predecessors (the bypass theory of change).

Handy guesses that some assumptions underlying our management concepts for at least 200 years will fail.

1. In the eighties and nineties concentration plus specialisation will not equal efficiency.
2. Labour, rather than being seen as a cost, will be regarded as an asset.
3. Hierarchy is no longer seen as natural. Obedience on its own does not work. Organisations will grow to communities and therefore our thinking has to shift about ownership and style of leadership, which should be earned rather than conferred.

In the future contractual organisations will be more efficient. Employees will be paid for work done, for output and not for time spent, for input. The contractual organisation, in which as much as possible is contracted out to individuals or to (semi) autonomous groups, is becoming more widespread. The focus of control changes from input and process to output that is contracted out.

In the management field Handy (1980) and Lievegoed (1977) expect more general management functions at a lower level, moving away from central organisation controlling all areas within the company. The management attitudes are shifting from risk avoidance towards risk taking.

THE INFORMATION MANAGEMENT CASE IN AN INDUSTRIAL ENVIRONMENT

In this section we will discuss the case of an engineering and construction company, confronted with the implementation of new information technology in the primary business functions. The intention was to move towards computer-integrated manufacturing, to improve operational, organisational and strategic responsiveness. It seeks to do this by integrating internal processes and external relations (with customers and suppliers), using new information technology. Restructuring established information and communication processes are a key factor in this integration. Therefore we have to consider the case from an information management perspective.

A profile of the company

The company is a job shopper for energy components and systems providing total energy systems and boilers for industrial applications. These are sold to the local public sector and private industrial firms, and on the world market. There are eight functional departments: marketing and sales; engineering; product development; manufacturing; finance and accounting; personnel; quality assurance; and organisation and automation. The company has 1,000 workers, mainly high skilled engineers and blue collar craftsmen.

Organisational framework and information strategy planning

The planning process for the computer-integrated manufacturing project used Information Systems Study (ISS), a methodology promoted by IBM. The project was organised by establishing a study team, consisting of two members of the board and six heads of department. Two external advisers were seconded to the study team to advise on information systems and CAD/CAM planning.

The study team developed a framework for analysing the existing information and communication flows. Working groups were created to analyse specific problem areas such as order acquisition, order processing, technical design, quality assurance, project planning, financial accounting and purchasing. Each of these working groups made an investigation and evaluation of the business processes and their informational relations in sessions conducted by an external consultant and a member of a study team.

The results of these sessions were detailed descriptions and evaluations of the existing business processes and information flows between the processes. On the basis of this work, the study teams selected eight information technology application areas. A working group was established for each of these areas, and given the job of carrying out feasibility studies, over a six-week period.

On the basis of these feasibility studies by the working groups, the study team formulated an information systems strategy and project plan. This went to the board of the company where it was approved.

This planning approach was primarily focused on the role of information and communication strategy planning, given the new capabilities of information technology. A subsidiary theme was the selection of specific automation projects like CAD and CAM.

Members of the study team were top managers; the working groups consisted of middle and low-level managers.

Case evaluation from an educational perspective

In evaluating managers' work in the field of information management, we will highlight some specific problem areas identified during the case study. The problem areas in the process of information strategy planning will be considered from an educational point of view.

Linking new information technology to corporate strategy and assessing the opportunities

Implementing new information technology in the primary business functions (Van Binsbergen, 1985) means innovation of processes and products with consequences for work structure and for the routing of horizontal and vertical information flows. It was very difficult for the managers in the case study company to get a global but consistent picture of possible new work structures and information flows. It was therefore very difficult for them to rate the new opportunities, in terms of their possible impact on corporate strategy.

Justification of opportunities became very arbitrary because of the lack of reliable data about the likely benefits of computerisation. Estimating the costs was much easier. Moreover, many of the benefits were relatively intangible; it was hard to establish quantitative links between expected benefits like more flexibility, shorter lead time, or better product quality *and* the corporate objectives.

Visualising new opportunities, their possible contributions to corporate strategy and their implications for existing structures is a very creative process. It is also a process which requires intensive interaction between different specialised managers. These tasks cannot be split between the different specialised management functions as the aspects are so heavily interrelated.

They require knowledge of the functional rather than technical properties of information technology and a more general 'boundary spanning' attitude from functionally specialised managers. It also requires a strategic, integrating way of thinking, which can relate information possibilities to tangible competitive advantage. How can their specialised function contribute to the added value of the company in the future?

Designing new information and organisational structures based on the new production structure

The managers found it difficult to think in terms of horizontal information flows and structures. They lacked the concepts to analyse and interpret the data collected about the existing horizontal, operational information flows. They had problems in understanding concepts like information data, data model, entities, structuring of data, etc. Managers prefer to think in authority lines and vertical information systems. Structured horizontal information flows crossing the borders of their areas of authority were a rather unknown issue in their work.

They also had problems in understanding dedicated methods for information analysis and design. This was the case where for example the team was required to relate information and organisational structures. Restructuring information flows often requires reshuffling organisational structures, otherwise you only 'speed up the mess'. The managers didn't have an overview of where application functions could be distinguished in different manufacturing environments.

Managing a business function requires general knowledge about (horizontal) information flows and structures and their interaction with the production structure and organisational structure (Galbraith, 1973). The manager needs concepts about types of computer applications and application portfolios and their fit in different organisational contexts. In spite of a short introduction programme there was still a lot of misunderstanding between the managers of the study team and the specialists because managers often missed knowledge about basic terms in computer science and informatics. The same could be said of the computer external specialists, who had problems in understanding the business and the organisation culture.

Structuring the implementation framework

In general, managers had problems with their role of structuring and managing the development of software. They lacked knowledge about the basic concepts of the software life cycle (phases, milestones, control of quality, budget, time documentation and project organisation).

Implementing new technology consists not only of developing software, but also a social-psychological process of changing the organisation. There was a lack of understanding of the interactions between developing *formalised* software and creating the *informal* conditions for social change.

In general there is an educational need for more concepts about the close interaction between technical, organisational and social features.

The case showed that commitment of people can be gained by participation of the low-level managers in the early stages of the planning process. Creating the right conditions, especially at the level of the high-skilled professional, is a crucial factor for successful implementation. Giving the people practical trials and experience in an experimental environment and opportunities to exchange experience with colleagues in other companies was a powerful tool in creating the changing conditions. These experiences were crucial in the decision-making process about computerisation in the primary business functions.

Some specific educational needs were 'how to do' knowledge about project management, standard software selection, communication skills and how to get software development accountable.

Selecting adequate specialists, consultants and services

Implementing new technology requires the use of temporary specialists and consultants. Managers often lack the knowledge and skills to select adequate specialists and consultants. To recruit the right person they lack the specific knowhow to define needs, their descriptions and required abilities and skills. In contracting consultants their specific knowledge of the information business was not sufficient to evaluate the bids.

In the field of acquiring computer services and hiring standard software the managers missed dedicated knowledge about contractual issues on, for example, legal and quality assurance matters. They were also unfamiliar with some of the financing (leasing, hiring) aspects.

A specific problem area for management was internal training of their labour force. There was a tremendous need for retraining; these investment costs were in absolute figures higher than the investment cost in hardware and software.

This training task was on a scale which the personnel manager had not faced before. There was a lack of understanding of the specific training needs and the possibilities in the education and training market for the approach and designing of training programmes.

THE NEED FOR NEW EDUCATIONAL MANAGEMENT CONCEPTS

By evaluating the case study we gained an impression of new management tasks in the area of information management facing the implementation of new information technology in the primary business functions. In the case study we focused on the managerial skills of *breakthrough*. We are convinced that after the implementation of new information technology there will be a need for quite different organisational forms and management *control* systems. In the implementation process a company has to anticipate these new forms of control.

I agree with Toffler and Handy's expectations that the future firm will be a constellation of flexible, rather autonomous small-community units framed in a network of interdependencies, regulating their interface by continuously adapted contracts. Clear boundaries between constellations and their environment do not exist. In a very dynamic environment the traditional bureaucratic system is no longer viable. This system, based on the belief that every problem has a matching component in the organisation — such as marketing, manufacturing or finance — only works when the types of problems are limited and repetitive. Today we see an increasing number of problems that cannot be neatly matched with one component of the organisation. It is for this reason I do not suggest the creation of a new specialised field of management: information management. I expect the existing pattern of specialised management functions will be heavily affected by new organisational forms like constellations.

Implementing the new information technology as a primary business function will be perhaps the beginning. For this reason we propose to create complementary information management education programmes in management education, upgrading the information management knowledge and skills of the functionally specialised managers. They could be a starting point for despecialising managers and (re)educating a new breed of more general boundary-spanning managers (*Outline for an Informatics Graduate Program*, 1985). Secondly we should try to integrate information management education modules in the existing undergraduate management education programmes.

REFERENCES

Galbraith, J.R. (1973) *Designing Complex Organizations*, Addison-Wesley, Reading, Mass.
Handy, C.B. (1980) 'Through the organizational looking glass', *Harvard Business Review*, Jan–Feb
Lievegoed, B.C.J. (1977) *Organisaties in ontwikkeling zicht op de toekomst*, Lemniscaat, Rotterdam
Outline for an Informatics Graduate Program (1985) Curriculum Committee Initiative Group, Informatics University, Holland
Toffler, A. (1984) *Preview and Premises*, Pan Books, London
——— (1985) *The Adaptive Corporation*, McGraw-Hill, Chicago
Van Binsbergen, P.R.M. (1985) 'CIM, een strategische benadering', *Informatie*, 27, 11
Wiseman, C. (1985) *Strategy and Computer: Information Systems as Competitive Weapons*, Dow Jones-Irwin, Homewood, Illinois

6

New Technology — New Problems: the Knowledge Gap Between Management and Computing

Barbara Rawlings

INTRODUCTION

This chapter reports from a study of a District Health Authority project to computerise personnel and patient records. The project is part of a national computerisation programme, and this is the first time in this district that non-manual record keeping and retrieval systems have been used.

The theme of the chapter is uncertainty; uncertainty which is embedded in the course of technical innovation and which has developed against a backdrop of traditional organisational structure. The uncertainties I describe here are maintained and often intensified by innovators' lack of technical knowledge. In Part One I will describe some of the features of technical innovation, and the uncertainty that surround these, and in Part Two I will develop a processual model of the development and maintenance of communication barriers between 'experts' and 'non-experts' who are involved in the innovation process. I will argue that because of the general lack of technical knowledge and a concomitant inability to recognise 'reliable' technical knowledge if it should appear, managers are working very much in the dark.

The uncertainties they experience make it very difficult for them to make decisions with confidence, to assess outcomes of decisions with detachment and to evaluate training needs rigorously. A central factor in all of these things is the existing National Health Service (NHS) organisational context, which generates additional complexities with regard to finance, pressure groups with varying degrees of influence. However, my concern in this chapter is to trace the micro-interactional processes of communication between innovating parties, and not to extend the analysis into the wider organisational structure of the NHS.

Figure 6.1: The organisation of the National Health Service

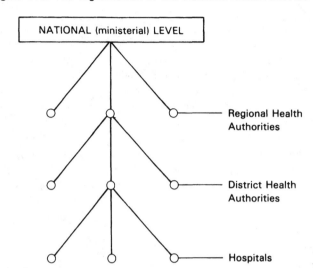

PART ONE

For reference here, the NHS organisational structure can be roughly represented as shown in Figure 6.1. Between 1984 and 1986, the District Health Authority in this study worked on a pilot study for an Integrated Personnel System (IPS), which combined employees' personnel files and payroll details, so that routine wages and salaries work could be facilitated. Since 1985 the district has been in the process of adopting and adapting a Patient Administration System (PAS) which was piloted elsewhere in the region, and which is intended to facilitate the administrative work involved in scheduling and organising the flow of in-patients and out-patients.

From the start, the Regional Health Authority elected to use internal skills and talent, rather than to employ specially trained computer personnel or to hire computer consultants to do the job for them. In line with this decision a regional project team was appointed, made up of administrative and clinical employees seconded from their posts, and various managers at district level were relieved of certain of their duties so that they could spend time on progressing computerisation. A target date was set, April 1987, by which time the whole region would be computerised, and a staggered timetable was drawn up so that districts would be at different stages at any one time.

As a researcher, I was struck by the notion that this huge organisation was prepared to spend millions of pounds on technology and systems it knew relatively little about, without taking steps to acquire an expertise in the field first. In discussion with colleagues involved in similar research, however, I have learned that this approach is quite common in both public and private organisations, and that decisions to buy equipment and decisions about which hardware and software to buy are frequently taken by managers who know relatively little about computer systems. In this paper I do not intend to debate the pros and cons of such a practice; my intention is rather to note that it has thrown the knowledge gap between management and computer specialists into relief in this organisation, and for this reason the knowledge gap is worth investigating in some detail.

Two different cultures

One way of delineating the subject matter of this paper is to briefly outline the views that hospital managers have of computer experts and the views that computer experts have of hospital managers. The distinction is a crude one, and the description of their viewpoints oversimplified, since people on each 'side' of the equation vary in respect of their technical knowledge and general preparedness to understand the other side's point of view. However, there are some general points that can be made to illuminate the views of each side on some contentious issues, particularly when these comprise the managers on the one hand and the associated hardware and software suppliers on the other.

The commercial relationship between buyers and sellers

The view from the NHS is this: NHS managers are aware of the lack of technical knowledge on their side, and aware that they have problems working out what they need in the way of hardware and software. One general view amongst the managers is that computer companies have taken advantage of this lack of knowledge to sell inappropriate hardware and software, to sell more than is needed, to overcharge and to insist on unfair penalty clauses. Specifically, companies are said to have made unrealistic bids for contracts, by falsely claiming that they could handle the complexity and scope of

NHS records systems.

The other side of the argument is this: the computer companies, far from feeling they have done well out of the NHS, point to a countrywide history of unmet contract dates, late payments, confused negotiations and unfounded allegations of liability. Apocalyptic stories of bad treatment by health authorities pass from mouth to mouth, and a number of companies are reported to be so concerned by the NHS approach that they do not now bother to tender for contracts.

Concepts of management systems

The view from the computer experts is this: their systems have advanced to such a state that they are not only able to help managers do their work more efficiently (i.e. do the work they currently do faster and more accurately), but their revolutionary ways of addressing problems are able to revolutionise the work itself. Unfortunately, the claim goes, management thinking is qualitatively outdated and the powerful opportunities for change afforded by the computer industry are not just unappreciated, they are not even understood in management circles.

The other side of the argument is this: managers see computer experts as generally disinterested in management problems and unwilling to spend time on working through them. Computer experts, say managers, believe only in their own logical systems, and cannot begin to appreciate the ordinary difficulties of real-life management activities. Management, say the managers, is mostly about people, and people are complicated beings to deal with. Computer experts, they claim, ignore this, and devise systems in which people are treated as if they are relatively unproblematic.

The accuracy of these claims is not an issue for this chapter. What is important is the nature and extent of the differences between the two outlooks. For the remainder of this chapter I want to explore aspects of the knowledge gap outlined here in more detail, and to suggest how this gap is created and maintained. I will begin by looking at what kinds of problems the knowledge gap causes for managers, and how managers resolve these problems. It will be helpful to lay out two types of problems: old and new.

Old problems

These are administrative matters that managers are well used to dealing with. They include requirements put upon local health authorities to carry out the decisions of higher central and regional bodies, by planning and executing policies to achieve regionally set aims and deadlines. As with other NHS major projects, the computerisation project requires financial resources, organisational restructuring, job redesign and room allocation. Ordinarily these requirements would present the management with complications, but the problems and the complications they present have many precedents: the authority and its hospitals are always short of money and space; there are always pressure groups in conflict over the use of these limited resources; organisational restructuring is always going to cause difficulties somewhere along the line, since it will suit some people and not others; job redesign is a notoriously unpopular phenomenon. Such problems then are not necessarily easy for managers to resolve, but they do at least have the advantage of having happened before. Since there are precedents, the parameters of the problems are reasonably clear and the moves towards solving them reasonably predictable.

New problems

With the advent of computerisation, managers have been presented with a whole set of new problems which they have never been asked to resolve before, such as how many terminals will be required, what kind of training will be needed and when and how the manual records should be transferred to computerised data. In addition, they have to resolve a number of matters which initially look like old problems (such as how much it will cost, where the money will come from and where the equipment will be sited) but which quickly lose their familiarity as the scale of uncertainties surrounding them becomes apparent. Managers cannot, for example, estimate costs with any degree of reliability, unless they have some idea of how much of everything they are likely to need. Thus the computerisation project has presented managers with a whole set of unfamiliar and unpredictable problems, which they do not have the skills and knowledge to resolve, but which they must resolve if the target date for computerisation is to be met.

This notion that the new problems of computer technology make it hard to solve familiar problems is worth examining in more detail. One essential planning task is to work out what is needed, but since the managers know very little about computer systems and equipment, they have major difficulties with this. A practical way of resolving the matter would be to rely on the advice of better informed people, but here there are the problems of working out who *is* better informed. To get back to the notion of two cultures, it is difficult for managers to know what equipment to order from suppliers, and how to assess the value of the information the suppliers give them. It is also difficult for the managers to know how much their fellow managers know about it, i.e. how to assess the claims to technical knowledge that their fellow managers make.

Over on the other side, it is difficult for computer suppliers to know what is going to be needed, since they do not have the knowledge of the size and complexities of the NHS organisation that the managers possess. They have to supply equipment and costings to people who (from the suppliers' point of view) do not know what they want. Thus neither the buyers, nor the sellers, really know what is going to be needed (although at various stages during the project they may think that they know) and this uncertainty is echoed right down to small-scale concerns, such as who is going to be responsible for what, where equipment is going to be sited, how often it is going to be used and who is going to do what work with it.

To explore in more detail what this means for managers, I want to examine the implications of dealing with problems for the 'first time ever'.

The first time ever

Everything that is being done on the project is being done for the first time ever. Even matters that look familiar turn out to be unfamiliar on closer inspection. For example, one major problem that threatened to hold up progress was the need to identify a site for the Central Processing Unit. Since space, like any other resource, is at a premium in the Health Service, the problem was predictably complicated, since it rapidly transpired that other pressure groups had the available space earmarked for their own needs. This complication had its precedents, however, and the problem did not initially look too difficult. However, one site after another was identified, investigated and discussed, only to be found wanting in some unexpected way: it was too far from some other building, too small, too dusty or too expensive to re-commission for computer use. All of these special requirements only became known to managers in the course of making decisions about the site; they were not known beforehand, although they became 'obvious' to everybody afterwards.

This 'first time ever' feature of the computerisation project is worth emphasising here, since it is so different from the routine familiarity of most management tasks. That is, managers cannot look to past experience to help them with this, nor can they recognise the shape and size of the problems they meet as readily or as accurately as they can do elsewhere. Unlike other projects and other decisions, computer decisions are made in the dark, and managers find out afterwards what the results are. Many things are deliberately left hazy (e.g. the type of training needed) because managers argue that they cannot know what will be needed until after they have tried. Outside assistance (e.g. the experience of districts that have already got similar systems up and running), is found to be only minimally helpful, since managers do not yet know enough about the systems to know what kind of help they need. Thus the managers are engaged in 'hands-on learning' in the classic sense of learning by doing, and by making their own mistakes.

There is then a high level of uncertainty about many aspects of the project, which manifests itself in various ways, as management problems. Two such problems will be discussed here: the open-ended commitment and the difficulties of evaluating expertise.

The open-ended commitment

Engagement in the project has become virtually an open-ended commitment for all concerned. As an example, three of the members of a steering group are Medical Records Officers. Throughout the history of the project, they have found themselves with extra work relating to computerisation, either work that is specifically to do with reordering patient administration data or work that is related in other ways, such as sitting on committees, attending meetings, explaining progress to subordinates or writing reports. This extra work is mostly done on top of their normal workload. At one meeting, the discussion turned to identifying 'computer reference people', i.e. named personnel who would be officially given the job of assisting computer users with the systems and sorting out any problems. One member of the meeting mentioned that in another district this work had been taken on by the Medical Records Officers. This brought an immediate chorus of loud protests from the Medical Records Officers present, who were adamant that they had taken on too much extra work already, and were unwilling to consider taking on any more.

A point to make here, which will surface again when I describe the communication problems that arise during the technical innovation stages, is that refusal to accept the open-ended nature of the commitment and to insist that work should be limited to what can be done during a day may be treated in this setting as evidence of 'technophobia', or as evidence of a personal inability to accept change. That is, during the innovation phase, managers may be seen as people who should be willing and able to alter their traditional workload by pruning and delegation: to do otherwise is to stand in the face of progress. Whether this is a just characterisation is not at issue here; what is important is that such characterisations are made and that they play a part in creating and maintaining particular kinds of technology-related differences between people. Such differences, as I will show later, help to generate communication problems which serve to further confuse the issues involved in technological innovation.

The open-endedness of the commitment is something which becomes apparent as time goes on, and which is evident at all levels for all people concerned. The project as a whole has taken longer, cost more and required more work than anyone expected at the outset. How much more work will be required is still not known. One aspect of the open-endedness of the commitment, however, which I will take up later in the chapter, is that it helps to breed suspicion. One question which managers and lower-level employees can ask themselves is: 'Did the senior management *really* not know how much all this was going to cost or *really* not know how much work it was going to be, or did they know all the time, and are only now telling us what we have let ourselves in for?'

Problems of evaluating expertise

Because the people involved in this project are managers rather than computer professionals, they do not know how to judge the technical knowledge of others. This is an essential point and partly explains the dilemmas managers have in hiring or buying computer expertise. If they employ systems analysts or computer consultants, how do they evaluate the quality of their work? How can they differentiate between good advice and bad advice?

Recently the District decided to appoint a computer manager.

Given that no one on the interviewing panel knew anything much about computer systems, the problem arose of how to assess candidates for this technical post. The post was considered to be a crucial one and the managers wanted to be sure they would choose someone who would suit their particular needs. They decided to co-opt a computer expert from outside to sit on the interviewing panel and help them in their task. This, however, faced them with almost exactly the same problem, one stage removed: how to choose an outside computer expert whom they could trust to represent their views. Although they felt they could trust one expert to assess another, they did not have enough technical knowledge to assure themselves of the suitability of the 'expert' for the panel.

The problem of judging the technical knowledge of others exists at all levels: how do District personnel evaluate the advice of managers from the Region, or how do they evaluate the ideas and comments of each other? In the next section I will show how managers involved in the project adopt practical means for resolving these issues, but I will argue that the knowledge gap is sustained and even enhanced by the use of these practical means. I will present this as a general picture of a process, and show how the creation and maintenance of the knowledge gap hinges on the difficulties any lay person experiences in evaluating other people's claims to possess knowledge with which they are personally unfamiliar, and on the existing status differences of the bureaucratic context in which project planning is carried out.

PART TWO

The creation and maintenance of the knowledge gap

Differential claims to possess knowledge

The lack of knowledge is presented not so much as a complete lack, but as a differential lack, i.e. when sitting in meetings it appears that some people know more than others (whether they actually do is another matter: what is important is that they appear to). When some people claim knowledge, and those that do not cannot assess the reality of the claims, then little gaps in their communication open up. Those who claim knowledge may also be accorded, or may claim, more rights to say what can and cannot be done. Those who do not claim this knowledge may feel they have fewer rights in this area. Pecking orders are formed in committees and meetings, and local beliefs about who to listen to and who not to listen to are erected and maintained. Those who claim to know, or who are believed to know, begin to talk in ways which others may find difficult to follow; those who claim to know begin to take certain things for granted (e.g. what the money should be spent on or what the ultimate aim of the project should be) so that these things become accepted as general common sense. Others, even if they wanted to, find it difficult to dispute some commonly accepted ideas because, as they and everybody else 'knows', they are ignorant of these matters and their comments are uninformed.

Thus a mystification process occurs, in which the knowledge required is defined by the people who claim to have it, and is more unattainable and mysterious than ever, since there are now inter-actional barriers between identifiable experts and lay people.

Knowledge claims and organisational power

One of the ways in which this mystifying process appears to be particularly powerful is when it is tied in with existing organisational status differences. That is, knowledge claims made by people with higher organisational status are particularly strong, since others may find it organisationally appropriate that such people should not only have more knowledge, but should also have more rights to define the parameters of debatable areas and more rights to make decisions.

With the addition of organisational power, claimants to knowledge can (wittingly or unwittingly) contribute to a further twist of the mystification process. This is when it is tied in with the apparent ability of more powerful people to 'pull strings' and to 'work behind the scenes'. A world is conjured up of people who know people, who can drop in a good word here and there, who owe each other favours, or who are somehow able to put pressure on others to get things moving when no amount of effort to do so has hitherto been successful. Thus in planning and steering meetings it sometimes happens that something which appeared as an insurmount-able problem at the last meeting has been unaccountably resolved. For example, the siting of the Central Processing Unit (CPU) was causing such difficulty that at one planning meeting it looked as though the target dates for completing the project could not be met, and that penalty clauses for late completion of contracts would be incurred from hardware suppliers. At the next meeting, it transpired that not only had the siting issue been resolved, but the contractors were already on site preparing the building for the installation of the CPU, and that all work was now running ahead of schedule.

Present in the meeting were people who already knew about this latest development, and people who were hearing about it for the first time. The matter was reported to the meeting, and a short discussion about what to do next was held between the people who already knew about it. The net effect of this was twofold: (i) it left those who had not known about it at a disadvantage, since they were not prepared for things to have moved on so far, and (ii) it effectively ended debate on certain issues which had not been resolved prior to the *fait accompli* of the 'work behind the scenes'. Thus the more powerful people in the room cut out and underlined what they regarded as important matters for resolution; whatever knowledge it was that they were basing this decision upon was clearly accepted by *them* as thoroughly sound, and any questions about whether that knowledge was *really* sound were no longer appropriate.

One of the results of this mystification process is a lessening of communication. Because some people now have knowledge and others have not, and because some of these claims to knowledge are tied to pre-existing organisational differences which already include communication barriers, those who still do not claim to possess knowledge begin to theorise about those who do as a substitute for actual communication, i.e. they begin to base their perceptions on belief and rumour rather than on first-hand experience. (This mirrors the ways in which managers theorise about computer experts and vice versa.)

This communication gap serves only to widen the knowledge gap between non-experts and experts (only now the 'experts' are the managers who have acquired knowledge and the 'non-experts' are those who have not). The process is circular and repetitive, as can be seen in Figure 6.2.

Along with this circular process goes a subsidiary process which springs from the freedom that non-communicants have to theorise about one another, and this is the development of suspicion, bad feeling and unhelpfulness. As an example, I have already outlined the beliefs that managers and computer experts hold about one another. At the day to day organisational level, the possibility that suspicion and bad feeling will develop is a matter for constant vigilance by management, who are greatly concerned to keep the confidence of the unions. Nevertheless, managers themselves are tied into this communication spiral, and they too develop and use their theories about other groups. Thus, for example, whilst the trade unions or other pressure groups theorise about management motives and aims, managers themselves develop theories about the

Figure 6.2: The maintenance of the knowledge gap as a communication process

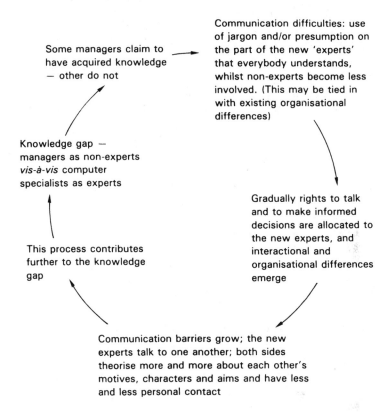

Some managers claim to have acquired knowledge — other do not

Communication difficulties: use of jargon and/or presumption on the part of the new 'experts' that everybody understands, whilst non-experts become less involved. (This may be tied in with existing organisational differences)

Knowledge gap — managers as non-experts *vis-à-vis* computer specialists as experts

Gradually rights to talk and to make informed decisions are allocated to the new experts, and interactional and organisational differences emerge

This process contributes further to the knowledge gap

Communication barriers grow; the new experts talk to one another; both sides theorise more and more about each other's motives, characters and aims and have less and less personal contact

motives and characters of groups who appear to be stubborn or unco-operative. Now that they have taken the plunge and begun to acquire computer knowledge and to accept the advent of new technology, they run the risk of becoming less tolerant of others who have not.

SUMMARY

In this chapter I have described the knowledge gap between management and computer experts, and shown how the gap manifests itself and is managed within the organisational context of the computerisation project.

I have indicated some of the ways in which people involved in the project come to believe that other people are more knowledgable and have more right to make decisions. I have also indicated the kinds of communication patterns and problems that occur over time during the project, and shown how these are closely related to the practical ways in which managers resolve the problems thrown up by their lack of computer knowledge.

If the knowledge gap between practitioners in any managerial field and the computer specialists they deal with is to be better understood, then some rigorous empirical research of such micro-interactional processes as these would be a good place to start.

CONCLUSION

At this point I would like to revise the notion of a 'knowledge gap'. Although the term is a useful way of introducing the topic of cultural, perspectival and interactional distances between the groups of people, it offers too simple a picture of the topic I have tried to outline here. The outstanding feature of the distance between the two groups is the problem of knowing what is required by the computerisation project, since managers do not know enough about computers and computer experts do not know enough about management. Whilst people adopt practical means of resolving problems as they arise, the practical judgements upon which they base their resolutions are born of managerial necessity rather than thorough knowledge of systems and needs.

From the evidence available it seems reasonable to note that simply to increase the availability and scope of technical training in the NHS would not in itself lift the general level of technical awareness or narrow the knowledge gap outlined here, since however the distribution of training is arranged there would still be a varied spread of technical proficiency in the organisation. A different approach aimed at equalising general stocks of technical knowledge, and raising the whole technical tone of the NHS managerial climate, may be more effective. The major problem for this and any other learning initiative in such a setting, however, is that any lead would have to be taken by managers who themselves are relatively unfamiliar with computing.

7

The Role of Computerised Information Systems in Developing Organisational Structure

Riitta Smeds

BACKGROUND

Business organisations are facing today a period of rapid 'computerisation' in almost all functions. Also the environment of organisations is changing due to new strategic possibilities of information technology. Computerised information systems are thus affecting organisational structure at multiple levels: they change the internal division of labour and the mechanisms of co-ordination, and they affect the strategies and the environment of the enterprise. Cumulative effects of these changes can lead the organisation into transition towards a new 'strategy-structure' configuration.

The purpose of this chapter is to analyse the development of organisational structure during the computerisation process. The research method is phenomenological (Sanders, 1982), since the evolution of one organisation is studied to explain its structural change during the period from its first computer application until today.

The evolutionary process approach has been chosen because cross-sectional contingency studies of 'computer impact' have yielded contradictory results (e.g. Whisler, 1970; Blau, Falbe, McCinley and Tracy, 1980; Mansour and Watson, 1980). Evolutionary studies are also called for in organisation theory (e.g. Kimberly and Miles, 1980; Miller and Friesen, 1982, 1984), and research on information systems implementation recommends an evolutionary framework as well (e.g. Robey, 1981; King and Kraemer, 1984).

Computerised information systems (CISs) have traditionally been seen as a new tool to reduce the analysable and quantitative uncertainty in the organisation. CISs have performed routine data processing and improved planning frequency. Other alternatives under growing uncertainty are, according to Galbraith (1972, 1977), strategic manoeuvring to reduce external interdependencies, the use of slack resources to reduce internal interdependencies, the use of lateral relations to enhance mutual adjustment between subsystems, or structural change towards self-contained clusters. The self-contained clusters multiply the possibilities of mutual adjustment within the clusters and simplify the intercluster co-ordination to standardisation of cluster outputs (Thompson, 1967). To co-ordinate the whole uncertainty reduction process of a complex organisation, standardisation of norms (also called organisational identity or culture) can be used as a 'meta-co-ordination mechanism' (e.g. van de Ven, 1986).

Since Galbraith's theoretical formulations CISs have evolved towards much greater decentralisation and integration possibilities. Also mutual adjustment can now be aided by CISs, and thus some of the qualitative (cause-effect) uncertainty (Daft and Weick, 1984; Daft and Lengel, 1986) can be reduced. Current CISs are new tools in the interdepartmental 'co-ordination package' of the organisation (Otley, 1980). But they give also new strategic possibilities to reduce environmental interdependencies (e.g. Ives and Learmonth, 1984; Porter and Millar, 1985).

In the development of organisations CISs are — besides being new tools — also sources of internal and external turbulence. Management can cope with this new uncertainty by making incremental CIS decisions building an emergent CIS-strategy or by a planned explicit CIS-strategy.

ORGANISATIONAL COMPLEXITY OF COMPUTERISED INFORMATION SYSTEMS

Computerised information systems can be classified in terms of their 'organisational complexity' (Ginzberg, 1975, 1979), their ability to handle reciprocal interdependencies and thus to support mutual adjustment and maybe to enhance cause-effect understanding. The classification is at the same time a chronological ordering of administrative CIS development (Kroeber, Watson and Sprague, 1980).

On the lowest level of organisational complexity of CISs are the routine, single-purpose basic data processing systems, automated report preparators, that do not change task relationships (e.g. payroll applications, accounts receivable and payable, historical reports).

They do not contain decision models, are batch updated, and their database is unique to the application. These systems can increase the quantity and frequency of information, but do not enhance cause-effect understanding. They are usually operated by lower management and clerks.

Integrated data processing systems co-ordinate multiple sequentially interdependent tasks within one function. They are single-purpose, preplanned batch-processing systems containing simple decision models (e.g. production scheduling, sales analysis, inventory control). Their database is common to applications within the system, and their outputs consist of scheduled summary reports of operational information. The systems can enhance the planning frequency, and previous manual planning is replaced by standardised input of data. Common operational data available in the database reduces some of the need for mutual adjustment within the department. Cause-effect understanding of the tasks is enhanced only if the users participate in the implementation process. After the implementation, the cause-effect relationships are 'hidden' in the programs. The users belong to lower management.

Information systems that link together several functions in a preprogrammed way can be called traditional management information systems (MISs) (e.g. production control, sales forecasting, budgeting). Their data can be processed by programmers interactively on a time-sharing basis. The systems contain management science models, which permits them to be used in what-if analyses (which are run by EDP personnel). The outputs are scheduled and 'on-demand' reports for middle management. Traditional MISs reduce planning effort that stems from sequential interdependencies between functions. Interdepartmental cause-effect understanding can increase through user participation in the implementation phase, and slightly through the use of simulations.

Basic data processing systems, integrated systems and MISs can be called transaction processing systems. They reduce quantitative and analysable uncertainty. Because of their preprogrammed nature, their implementation must be managed as a planned change project (e.g. Ginzberg, 1975).

Current systems with decision support emphasis have potential also to enhance cause-effect understanding and aid in mutual adjustment, which means a higher organisational complexity. They can be developed in a flexible, evolutionary way (e.g. Carlson and Sprague, 1982).

Multipurpose systems for managerial decision-making are called decision support systems (DSSs). They become possible with the advent of microcomputers, which had enough individual data processing and memory capacity and which could also be integrated to larger data and model bases. DSSs are not preprogrammed, but contain flexible, non-procedural tool programs (sometimes called fourth-generation languages) for data processing, and a user-friendly interface (menus, etc.) for retrieval analysis and transfer of data. In contrast to the preprogrammed CISs, DSSs can be developed in an evolutionary way, prototyping the applications and linking them to integrated networks together with other micros, minicomputers or mainframes. The applications contain management optimisation models, which still are in algorithmic form.

Non-integrated micros are not yet DSSs. They are not organisationally complex, since they only integrate subtasks of one person (so-called integrated work environment consisting of word processing, spread-sheet calculations, project management, data management, etc.). However, they can enhance the individual cause-effect understanding. They can also be used to substitute old basic data processing systems and even the smaller integrated data processing systems.

With the integration of micros into networks to share facilities (printers, disk memory), and even data and applications, the organisational (and technical) complexity of the system grows and it can be called a DSS. The common databases, which can be also external to the organisation, are used interactively by managers. Sometimes also applications in a model base are shared. This requires data and communication standards, and also the EDP knowledge in the organisation must be standardised (Methlie, 1983). But in exchange for this standardisation, the DSS can reduce, in addition to sequential, also reciprocal interdependencies: with the electronic transfer of data and messages, the need for human interaction for mutual adjustment under prevailing uncertainty is reduced.

Expert systems are a new generation of DSSs that process natural language routine 'expert data'. In effect, all standards, rules and policies of the organisation are this kind of knowledge, and thus potential contents of expert systems. Some business expert systems are already available for microcomputers. Expert systems consist of a knowledge base of 'rules of the thumb' (inference rules), of a database with situational facts and of an inference engine, which employs the rules to interpret the facts. The reasoning can be shown to the user (backward reasoning), and rules may be modified in the light of new experience. The design of 'programs' can thus be conducted by trial and error of logical rules, as an alternative for algorithmic specifications of the older generation CISs (D'Agapeyeff, 1983).

Besides the administrative applications, computers are also used as technological tools: from simple calculation and programming applications to sophisticated CAD and CAE, which already require integration to printer facilities, to a central database and often to administrative CISs (e.g. production control). Thereby their organisational complexity increases.

As the local processing capacity in microcomputers grows, the systems are moving into a new development cycle: mainframes are specialising in mass processing, batch applications and management of large databases. Minicomputers specialise in data management and communication (linking together micros). Previous 'integrated systems' and MISs are transferred to superminis. Processing is more and more decentralised to microcomputers that are used as workstations of the minis. The EDP-architecture is moving towards a two- or three-level structure: micros integrated directly to mainframe, or micros integrated first at an intermediary level (to a micro network, to a central micro or a mini) and then to a mainframe (Hannus and Mäkelin, 1983).

The central CIS-feature from the organisations' point of view are the integration possibilities. They depend on network solutions that are technically difficult and also expensive. Local area networks that would connect a wide range of systems and devices from different suppliers have not yet been developed, so the organisations are tied to a few suppliers and to new generation hardware to achieve system integration. Those pioneering organisations that have developed their own tailored computer systems with old technology are at a disadvantage when compared with skilful followers, who can leap-frog into the compatible integrated information networks of today.

BACKGROUND TO THE CASE

The case organisation is a Nordic high-technology enterprise. It was founded by a scientist about 50 years ago, on the basis of a scientific discovery that led to a unique product innovation. Internalised technological knowhow and high-quality products have been the key success factors of the enterprise during its whole development.

The high rate of innovation (unanalysability) has required an organic and flexible structure that has relied in its co-ordination

75

Table 7.1: The computerised information systems introduced in the case organisation

Type of system	Year	Application area
A. Technological tools		
Non-integrated microcomputers	1974	R&D programming
Non-integrated microcomputers	1974	PRODUCTION processing of quality data
Non-integrated minicomputer	1978	R&D programming
Micro-network	1979	R&D (product-line) programming
Non-integrated microcomputers (new generation)	1979	PRODUCTION processing of quality data
Non-integrated CAD-system	1981	R&D hardware design
Non-integrated minicomputer	1982	R&D programming
B. Administrative systems		
Non-integrated microcomputer	1979	MARKETING (technical service) word processing
Basic data procesing system	1979	FINANCE wage accounting
Minicomputer used as shared processor for office automation (non-integrated systems)	1980	Word processing
	1981	link to external data base
	1982	own scientific data base
	1983	telex
Management information system	1982	FINANCE accounting and budgeting
Management information system	1983	PRODUCTION inventory and production control
Non-integrated microcomputers (also as terminals to minicomputer)	1984	ORGANISATION-WIDE administrative functions word processing, spread-sheet applications

mainly on 'high-tech identity' and mutual adjustment. The organisation did not even have a formal organisation chart for the first 25 years. With growth in volume a simple functional structure was formed.

During the ten-year period the enterprise implemented all of its computerised information systems (see Table 7.1). The case is an example of an emergent EDP-strategy that grew out of the organisation's critical external interdependencies, i.e. its product innovations.

SETTING THE SCENE FOR STRUCTURAL DEVELOPMENT

The functional organisation of 1975 was quite small and operated in a turbulent high-technology environment. The market was interpreted as saturated, and did not promise growth. Therefore the organisation searched actively for new product innovations. The incorporation of information technology into the main product created spinoff innovations that became the seeds for new business. Electronic data processing knowledge began to accumulate in the research and development department, where the software for the products was programmed.

To co-ordinate the search for new business and the choice of new products on the strategic level, a formal business planning framework with special emphasis on innovation, flexibility and growth was created. Interfunctional *ad hoc* meetings were organised on top management level to formulate product policy and to help in the search for new business ideas. Financial control was performed manually through a rolling budgeting process and accounting procedures. The frequency of operational planning was three months. The organisational handbook was updated to standardise common procedures into policies and instructions.

In the R&D department innovations required mechanisms to reduce qualitative uncertainty. The co-ordination mechanism remained, as before, mutual adjustment in teams and projects. Production was planned to inventory on the basis of sales forecasts. It was co-ordinated by standards, rules and a manual planning system developed by materials administration. The marketing function was differentiated by geography and product. Internal co-ordination relied mostly on standardisation of skills. Personal customer contacts, technical service and user training were critical external interdependencies, which caused qualitative uncertainty and required mutual adjustment skills. The finance department was organised as a small central administration office. In all functional departments (except finance), weekly co-ordination meetings were also held.

Interdepartmental co-ordination required specially scheduled meetings. Marketing and production integrated their forecasts and production plans through meetings every three months. To co-ordinate the critical interdependencies between R&D, marketing and production (mainly product quality), a series of design reviews for new products was created. Quality control was decentralised into the production department, and the processing of quality measurement data was the first EDP application outside R&D. It was programmed by R&D and implemented on non-integrated microcomputers on the shop floor.

Thus the accumulation of EDP knowledge in the organisation began in a decentralised manner in R&D and in the production function. No EDP department existed, and no explicit EDP strategy either.

The first structural transition in 1976 was initiated by co-ordination differences in production. The main product consisted of a 'system part' produced in single units or in small batches, and of 'complementary parts' produced in large batches. The differences in production control between these two production modes led to the idea of differentiation into two production lines already in 1975. This differentiation spread also to R&D and marketing by 1976, because of significant changes in product technology and of the resulting new business idea that required its own product line. The organisation structured itself into a decentralised partial matrix consisting of three product lines (partial meaning here that the matrix lacked product line managers). The new business did not have a dedicated production department, but was served by the old production function.

THE PARTIAL MATRIX (1976-9)

During the partial matrix structure, the differentiation according to technology and clients was driven further. Product manager roles were founded in the product lines, but functional influence was still dominant. To enhance the capability to deal with the multiplied external interdependencies, an integrating department was created in marketing (technical services). In addition to the decentralised R&D departments, a centralised R&D staff was maintained.

To co-ordinate the overall learning process of the decentralised organisation in the direction of qualitative uncertainty reduction, significant training of the personnel was begun. Training in creativity, co-operation and quality were means to maintain the high-tech identity and to improve innovation and mutual adjustment skills.

Incremental computerisation continued. In R&D, a minicomputer was installed. The applications were software development for a new generation of the main product. The system was originally low in organisational complexity, but developed later (in the matrix

Figure 7.1: The accumulation of EDP knowledge in the case organisation

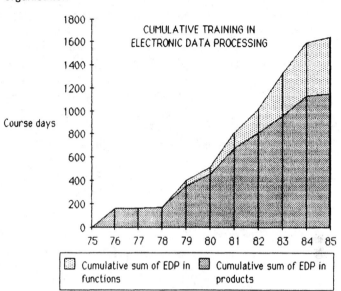

phase) into a more integrated configuration: excess computer capacity could be used via terminals for word processing and for an internal database of scientific references.

The differentiation of R&D was reflected also in the CISs: the new products needed their own type of software development, and a separate micro-network was installed in the new product line.

A new generation of microcomputers was installed in the production departments to improve quality tests and analyses of the new products. They were decentralised, non-integrated systems, which rationalised testing and gave better operational quality control information.

The first non-integrated word processing system for high-quality customer documents was purchased in the technical service department.

The partial matrix was a period of EDP knowledge development in R&D and production, tightly connected with information technology in the product. In spite of first word processing applications, the accumulation of administrative EDP knowledge for coordination purposes had not begun. The development of the EDP 'knowledge base' in the organisation is depicted in Figure 7.1.

THE MATRIX STRUCTURE (1979–84)

After three years in a partial matrix, the growing product lines demanded full-time product line managers, and the organisation changed into a matrix structure. The already frequent co-ordinative meetings were multiplied, because each meeting got its functional and product-line equivalent. The ripe matrix had around 700 scheduled meetings per year, and innumerable *ad hoc* arrangements. The matrix was a period of rapid growth and learning.

Mutual adjustment was clearly the main means of co-ordination, and personnel training developed the required skills. But also the old planning procedures were maintained, and policies and instructions grew in number. A quality integrator was appointed to the central administration, and the quality system was integrated into a comprehensive set of manuals, differentiated by function and product line.

Computerisation continued in the matrix phase in an emergent way. For the first time initiatives for CISs came also from administrative and co-ordination needs. In finance a basic data processing system for the routine accounting of wages and salaries was purchased. Also a sophisticated foreign MIS for accounting and budgeting was acquired, since the manual accounting system was getting overloaded by the dual control needs of the matrix. Both of these administrative applications were used as non-integrated, centralised batch processing systems with external computer utilities, and they were operated by a minimum of personnel in central administration.

The accounting and budgeting MIS was purchased 'off the shelf', and no formal implementation project was founded, since the system was supposed to be a standard package. The implementation took over two years. Learning progressed slowly through trial and error, even though a planned change approach was needed. (For example, exact operational cost information was missing for about two years, since the manual accounting system was discarded too early.) After one year of turbulence the first EDP expert in finance was hired. The excellent EDP knowhow that had accumulated in R&D and was developing in production had not been used in finance, since administrative applications were regarded as secondary. Until today, only a small part of the comprehensive package is used as an 'integrated data processing system', although the system could in principle be used even in a decentralised DSS manner.

During the matrix period, an MIS to control small batch production (i.e. the production of the 'system parts' of products) was implemented. It was based on a tailored software package, an in-house minicomputer and micros as terminals to allow decentralised use. The implementation process was a planned change project with user participation, managed by a system specialist in materials administration. The system was flexible and user friendly (containing menus and what-if analyses). Its main features were capacity planning and inventory control, and it produced common product data for marketing and R&D.

Both the accounting and production CISs were already organisationally quite complex. They were substitutes for interdepartmental manual planning, which now became partly automated into standardised data input and preplanned programs. The operational planning frequency did not increase although the systems would have allowed it (the critical success factor was not internal efficiency, but flexibility and innovation).

Human information processing 'links' were needed to integrate these separate systems, since no computer network existed. Sometimes unofficial individual micro applications were developed to mend gaps in electronic integration. One example of this is a microcomputer-based spread-sheet program for financial consolidation and what-if analyses, which was used instead of the rigid centralised accounting system.

Because the systems were implemented in the matrix phase, they both contained a centralised database of functional and product line information. This was an important feature in the future structural development of the organisation.

Office automation progressed in the matrix phase. Terminals were linked to the R&D minicomputer for word processing and telex, and a link to an international scientific database was established. Personal stand-alone microcomputers were purchased in all parts of the organisation. In addition to individual applications, they could also be used as terminals for the production-CIS. This was the first integrative feature in the computerisation process, and it emerged as a side-effect of the successful production-CIS project.

In R&D, a non-integrated CIS for computer-aided design of hardware was implemented. Also a new and more effective minicomputer for software development was purchased (this allowed the office automation applications in the older mini). The R&D systems were not integrated to the production system, although they used partly the same data. The optimal technical requirements of the

R&D systems were more sophisticated than those of the production system, which made networking impossible.

THE DIVISIONAL STRUCTURE (1984–)

The technological and marketing differences of the product lines had grown further and a fourth product line had been founded. Many important tasks (especially production) were still organised centrally, which caused priority conflicts. The need for more flexibility and mutual adjustment around the new businesses was solved by a divisional structure.

The organisation as a whole could now be co-ordinated more by standardisation of division output. The importance of organisation-wide rules diminished, and planning became more informal, especially in the new business divisions. The old business preserved its rather formal structure. Inside the new divisions the structure consisted of functional units, combined into teams and projects. The overall 'meta-coordination' of the organisation towards an innovative identity was supported through intensive internal training.

The most complex CISs (accounting and production systems) allowed the structural transition to take place easily, because of their centralised databases that contained all the data needed for divisional control. The production planning system could also be used decentrally. All other CISs were non-integrated applications and could be easily regrouped in the transition.

CONCLUSIONS

The computerisation process of the case enterprise developed in an evolutionary learning-by-doing manner, which is consistent with the enterprise's innovative strategy. EDP was considered a tool mainly for qualitative uncertainty reduction when incorporated into new product innovations. The role of analysable, quantitative uncertainty reduction was secondary, and a rigid EDP strategy was consciously avoided. The organisation did not have an EDP department, not even an integrator or an explicit EDP policy.

This lack of CIS-inertia has on the one hand allowed for the rapid structural transitions of the enterprise. But on the other hand, different subsystems of the organisation have developed their CISs rather autonomously and without consideration of integration possibilities. This causes a new problem of inertia, if the enterprise in the future aims to reduce uncertainty and gain efficiency through data or applications sharing in its computerised information systems.

REFERENCES

Blau, P.M., Falbe, C.M., McCinley, W. and Tracy, P.K. (1980) 'Technology and organization in manufacturing', in Katz, D., Kahn, R.L. and Adams, J.S. (eds), *The Study of Organizations*, Jossey-Bass, San Francisco, pp. 14–32

Carlson, E.D. and Sprague, R.H. (1982) *Building Effective Decision Support Systems*, Prentice-Hall, Englewood Cliffs, NJ

Daft, R.L. and Lengel, R.H. (1986) 'Organizational information requirements, media richness and structural design', *Management Science*, 32, 5 (May), 554–71

Daft, R.L. and Weick K.E. (1984) 'Toward a model of organizations as interpretation systems', *Academy of Management Review*, 9, 2, 284–95

D'Agapeyeff, A. (1983) *Expert Systems, Fifth Generation and UK Suppliers*, NCC Publications, National Computing Centre, Manchester

Galbraith, J.R. (1972) 'Organization design: An information processing view', in Lorsch, J.W. and Lawrence, P.R. (eds), *Organization Planning. Cases and Concepts*, Richard D. Irwin and Dorsey Press, Homewood, Ill., pp. 49–74

—— (1977) *Organization Design*, Addison-Wesley, Reading, Ma.

Ginzberg, M.J. (1975) 'A process approach to management science implementation', Dissertation, Massachusetts Institute of Technology

—— (1979) 'A study of the implementation process', in Doktor, R., Schultz, R.L. and Slevin, D.P. (eds), *The Implementation of Management Science*, TIMS Studies in the Management Sciences, 13, North-Holland Publishing Company, Amsterdam, pp. 85–102

Hannus, J. and Mäkelin, M. (1983) *Mikrotietokoneet yrityksessä*, (Microcomputers in the Enterprise, in Finnish), Amer-Yhtymä Oy, Weilin+Göösin kirjapaino, Espoo

Ives, B. and Learmonth, G.P. (1984) 'The information system as a competitive weapon', *Communications of the ACM*, 7, 2 (December), 1193–201

Kimberly, J.R. and Miles, R.H. (1980) *The Organizational Life Cycle*, Jossey-Bass, San Francisco

King, J.L. and Kraemer, K.L. (1984) 'Evolution and organizational information systems: An assessment of Nolan's stage model', *Communications of the ACM*, 27, 5 (May), 466–75

Kroeber, D.W., Watson, H.J. and Sprague, R.H. (1980) ' An empirical investigation and analysis of the current state of information systems evolution', *Information & Management*, 3, 35–43

Mansour, A.H. and Watson, H.J. (1980) 'The determinants of computer based information systems performance', *Academy of Management Journal*, 23, 3, 521–33

83

Methlie, L.B. (1983) 'Organizational variables influencing DSS-implementation', in Sol H.G. (ed.), *Processes and Tools for Decision Support*, North-Holland Publishing Company, Amsterdam, pp. 93–104

Miller, D. and Friesen, P.H. (1982) 'The longitudinal analysis of organizations: A methodological perspective', *Management Science*, 28, 1013–34

——— (1984) *Organizations: A Quantum View*, Prentice Hall, Englewood Cliffs, NJ

Otley, D.T. (1980) 'The contingency theory of management accounting: Achievement and prognosis', *Accounting, Organizations and Society*, 5, 4, 413–28

Porter, M.E. and Millar, V.E. (1985) 'How information gives you competitive advantage', *Harvard Business Review*, July–August, pp. 149–60

Robey, D. (1981) 'Computer information systems and organization structure', *Communications of the ACM*, 24, 10 (October), 679–87

Sanders, P. (1982) 'Phenomenology: A new way of viewing organizational research', *Academy of Management Review*, 7, 3, 353–60

Thompson, J.D. (1967) *Organizations in Action*, McGraw-Hill, New York

Van de Ven, A.H. (1986) 'Central problems in the management of innovation', *Management Science*, 32, 5 (May), 590–607

Whisler, T. (1970) *The Impact of Computers on Organizations*, Praeger, New York

8

Constructing Organisational Forms for Flexible Computing

Howard Rose

INTRODUCTION

Recent advances in computer information technologies seem to pose something of a dilemma for managers. The widespread diffusion of computer applications has created the potential for interlinking and integrating computer systems which, in turn, has suggested opportunities for greater centralisation. By contrast, the reducing costs of microcomputers and computing power generally, the development of simpler programming languages, and especially the appearance of a wide range of software packages, have contributed to an explosion of informal, end-user and personal computing. This latter phenomenon is potentially a strong countervailing pressure to the previously mentioned centralising tendencies, by virtue of the demands for autonomy and individual initiative generated by users.

CENTRALISED VERSUS DECENTRALISED COMPUTING

The debate surrounding the merits or otherwise of centralised versus decentralised organisation structures for computing is a long-standing one, which certainly goes back as far as Leavitt and Whisler (1958). Whilst the goal has always been to identify the most appropriate organisational form, a universally appropriate arrangement has not been found. One reason for this may be that the debate is actually rooted in more basic issues of organisation structure and behaviour. As King has put it, 'Changing technology merely rearranges the forum in which these issues are debated' (1983, p. 320). Some of the more recent developments in computing technologies and the potential implications which their novel features have for management organisation have been discussed by Child (1984).

In a review of the earlier empirical literature, Robey (1977) concluded that the management structure of an organisation was not primarily influenced by the use of computer information technologies, but rather by the nature of the task environment. Computer technologies, he suggested, should be treated as a moderating variable that could be moulded to support either centralised or decentralised management structures. He did propose, however, that greater centralisation was associated with relatively stable or simple task environments, whilst decentralisation was associated with more complex or dynamic task environments. Finally, he pointed to the difficulty of trying to assess the overall impact of computerisation on management structure, where there is a wide variety of uses of computer systems within an organisation.

The notion of computer technology as a moderating, rather than an independent, variable has been applied by Robey (1981) to some further empirical studies. Here the effect of the implementation of computer information systems (CIS) on organisation structure was examined, with respect to the degree of centralisation of authority and control and the extent of lateral co-ordination. Again the conclusion drawn is that computer technology is a moderating variable. In a more recent discussion of CIS design and organisational change, Robey (1983) has proposed that the notion of computer technology as a moderating variable is also inadequate. Such an approach, he suggests, neglects the active role of human designers in the design of computer systems and organisational structures. Whilst this recognition of human choice is welcome, there is a sense in which Robey tends to adopt a too rationalistic view of the relationship between design objectives and organisational outcomes.

The tendency for commentators to adopt a too rationalistic viewpoint is pointed out by King (1983), in a comprehensive review of the debate over centralised versus decentralised computing. The result is that insufficient attention is given to the effect of the 'politics of organisation and resources' on the choice of organisational arrangements. Concerning the main dimensions of available options, King delineates three main aspects of centralisation. Control, he suggests, is the crucial aspect and is concerned with the locus of decision-making in the organisation. The other two aspects, physical location (concerned with the siting of facilities) and function (concerned with the position of activities or responsibilities within the organisation structure), are subordinate to the question of control. The options available with respect to these three aspects are extreme centralisation, extreme decentralisation or some intermediate arrangements.

The managerial challenge, says King, is to find an arrangement that meets user needs (including the opportunity to experiment), without writing a blank cheque or creating problems for overall management control. The primary discriminator is therefore between corporate and user department needs. In choosing an option, the fundamental question is who will have control over procurement, use and management of computing technologies. That question must be answered by central management and be based on an evaluation of existing arrangements. It should also recognise the drive towards end-user computing and take account of the politics of organisation. With regard to the latter, whilst mixed strategies or the adoption of intermediate arrangements may often produce compromise solutions, they do not eliminate the root causes of centralisation disputes. Rather, they allow the acknowledgement of diverse interests and provide the means for giving users some of what they want, whilst also securing a degree of commitment to corporate organisational objectives.

In the discussion referred to earlier, Child (1984) proposes that new information technologies extend the possibilities for managerial control, have considerable potential for facilitating integration within management, and permit a novel degree of physical dis-aggregation of work locations. The question that this raises, suggests Child, is the appropriateness of prevailing structures of centralisation and delegation within organisations. According to Child, the evidence in Britain is that the centralisation option is being chosen, encouraged by competitive and financial pressures. It is also being assisted by the availability of information and decision support brought about by the new information technologies.

There is, however, no overwhelming reason, Child argues, why information technologies cannot be used to facilitate more effective delegation. There is also considerable potential for IT to reverse the growth trend in managerial and related overheads in three main areas. First, office automation presents opportunities for economies in clerical and secretarial staff. Second, IT can facilitate moves towards simpler and smaller management structures. Third, the spread of personal computing and networking raises doubts about the continuation of large centralised computing departments and suggests a reappraisal of their role. This latter point, in particular, raises questions about the management of computing services themselves.

Some of these questions have been addressed by Webb (1985) in a discussion of the growing demand within organisations for direct access to computing power and computerised information by users, including managers. His discussion focuses on five guidelines to managers to enable the development of flexible computing facilities. These guidelines include reference to decentralising facilities for informal computing, thinking in terms of networks rather than hierarchies and making summary information from formal databases available to informal users. Perhaps the most significant of the guidelines is the one which encourages the setting up of arrangements for servicing and managing informal computing. This concern arises from the view that traditional centralised computing is unable to respond rapidly and flexibly to informal user demands. In turn this has been seen to lead to a proliferation of a host of incompatible types of equipment and systems.

The logic of the guidelines proposed by Webb is that the utilisation of current technological developments can facilitate the decentralisation of much computing activity and reduce the dependence on mainframe systems. This in turn suggests the possibility of reassigning systems analysts who are no longer required for development work on formal systems, to a support role for informal users. The implications are wide-ranging. For example, it opens up the possibility of formally transferring systems analysts to user departments so that their allegiance is to those departments and they are carried on those departments' budgets. It raises the issue of how to provide the links between these user-dedicated specialists so that ideas are shared and work is not duplicated. It also raises the matter of the role of the central computing department and the extent to which it should control the overall development of computerisation.

In their different ways systems integration and end-user computing have contributed to the dilemma facing managers as they seek to find ways to manage computing services and systems. The issue may be posed in terms of a search for organisational forms which strike a balance between maintaining centralised control and providing decentralised facilities. Without wishing to press the point too hard there is a similarity here to Peters and Waterman's (1982) discussion of 'simultaneous loose-tight properties' in organisational structures. Whilst this may not be a new problem for organisations, the rapid developments in the scale and range of computer applications perhaps now poses it in a new and acute form.

SOME EMPIRICAL FINDINGS

The following discussion arises from studies that the author is currently carrying out, part of which are concerned with the organisational arrangements for managing computerisation and computing services. The preliminary findings suggest that some trends are emerging in the development of these organisational forms. The findings reported here come from studies of six firms engaged in various industrial and commercial activities. They include firms engaged in the:

— manufacture of electronic components
— manufacture of computer equipment
— design and manufacture of heating and ventilating systems
— manufacture of pharmaceuticals
— retailing of do-it-yourself goods
— selling of insurance services

Some of these firms had introduced computer technologies fairly recently, whilst others had been using them for many years. Even though the computer applications varied considerably, there were a number of similarities in the issues related to computerisation that these firms were currently addressing. The aim here is to outline some of the main findings of these studies. For convenience of presentation it will be useful to consider the six cases with respect to two organisational variables. First, the degree of central or devolved provision of computing facilities and computing expertise. Second, the extent and manner of control over computer developments and the hardware and software standards for computer systems. Examined in this way, there are important variations in the organisational solutions adopted.

The degree of centralised or devolved provision was the area where the firms varied considerably. The two most extreme examples were the insurance firm and the heating and ventilating firm. The insurance firm is a classic example of Robey's finding that centralised provision of computing facilities was associated with a simple primary task. The main use of computer systems in this firm was for the administration of client policies and these systems were provided on a local area network, based on three interlinked minicomputers, within the firm's head office. The establishment of this central core had developed out of a consultant's report which had recommended a high degree of centralisation.

89

The firm's 30 local offices throughout the country did not have terminals giving them access to these central computer systems and, for those offices, computerisation meant that they had to adopt standardised procedures and formats for their records. Local offices simply filled out forms with clients' details and forwarded these daily to head office, where they were processed. However, the local offices each had three or four microcomputers providing word processing and spreadsheet facilities, networked to a mainframe computer in the firm's parent company. The decision to adopt these facilities and to extend them was made centrally. Future plans to develop office automation and link microcomputers into a new head office mainframe were part of the same strategy, which was seen to be a way of enabling local autonomy as well as centralised systems.

Like the provision of computing facilities, the provision of computing expertise was also centralised within head office. Although the largest proportion of computing staff consisted of computer operators, there was a small group of analysts and programmers providing technical support for users within head office. The significant points to be made about this case are that the primary task, as mentioned, was relatively simple, the firm had computerised within the last five years and with 400 employees was not particularly large. These factors may be seen as facilitative of this centralised approach to the provision of computing facilities and expertise.

Organisational control over computing was vested in the central computing department. Broad objectives were set by the department for user developments and there were established procedures for handling proposals for computer developments. Decisions about development proposals were the responsibility of the computer manager, although the user department had the right of appeal to a regular management meeting if not satisfied. Similarly, the scheduling of development work was the responsibility of the computer department although the users would be deeply involved in the acceptance testing. Overall, the situation described could be considered to represent a form of *de facto* tight control, based on the centralisation of computing facilities and expertise. The continuation of this situation could depend on the ability to continue providing a satisfactory level of service to users, as the facilities for informal computing expanded.

The heating and ventilating firm provided some interesting points of contrast. In particular, its current involvement with computer systems had only begun towards the end of the 1970s although it had

had a previous experience with computer systems in the 1960s. This latter experience strongly influenced its current approach to computerisation. This firm was relatively large and had several lines of business located at several sites in the UK. Computing facilities were divided into three main areas of activity, namely production, technical support and administration.

Administrative applications dealt with standard functions such as accounting, payroll and other financial records. These administrative systems were run on a mainframe computer, networked to two minicomputers with associated work stations. Technical services utilised approximately 30 microcomputers for carrying out various technical calculations using both bought-in packages and some in-house programs, as well as two minicomputers for computer-aided design. Several of the microcomputers were networked to a mainframe installation in production.

The strategy underlying this firm's approach is instructive because it illustrates how an organisation can learn from its experience. In the early 1960s this firm had moved to its present location from another area and had installed a large mainframe computer for its production operations, which provided a sophisticated but not very flexible production control system. This installation was run by a sizeable group of computer staff. The inflexibility of the system led a few years later to the board, at the instigation of the managing director, deciding to remove the computer and close down the computer department, on the grounds that the computer was telling the company how to run the business rather than the other way around. The experience created a deep antipathy amongst the members of the board to the use of computer systems within the firm. From the late 1960s onwards any large-scale data processing was farmed out to a computing bureau, although manual systems used within the firm continued to be based on a computerised format.

In response to pressures for computer systems, particularly for specialised technical applications, consultants were brought in towards the end of the 1970s to advise on computerisation. On the consultants' recommendation three mainframe computers were installed initially, but then reduced to one when the usage did not justify all three. The strategy had evolved subsequently to put greater emphasis on devolved computing rather than centralised provision. It was expected that when the single large mainframe for administrative systems was replaced it would be replaced by another minicomputer to increase the capacity of the network. The

91

underlying theme was that it was the needs of the business that were important and that nothing should develop by a 'computer logic' until the benefit to the business could be proved to the satisfaction of the board.

Perhaps the most significant aspect of this firm's approach was that there were only two formally designated computing specialists within the whole firm. One of these was responsible for the technical services side and worked to the technical director, whilst the other was responsible for the administrative side and worked to the financial director. Apart from them, all software was either bought in or developed by users, for whom programming courses were made available. Similarly, hardware and software maintenance was part of a contract agreement with the local supplier. As one might expect, control over computerisation in this firm was tight. But it is important to consider the form of that tight control to appreciate its relationship to the devolved provision of computer facilities.

Overall responsibility for computerisation had been given to the technical director a few years previously. He chaired a co-ordinating committee for computerisation which had been established within the past year. The committee had come about in response to the perceived tendency to fragmentation in the firm's approach to computerisation and the growing number of requests to the managing director for authority to computerise various functions. One of the first tasks for the committee after being set up was to produce policy guidelines for electronic data processing. Its subsequent role was to monitor and review existing systems, to evaluate proposals for new systems, and to oversee in-house training for computing. Concerning software standards, all in-house programs had to be written in a specified language and log books kept for all programs written. Microcomputers used in technical applications were restricted to products of one manufacturer to comply with the servicing contract.

Proposals from users, particularly for technical applications, were examined by the co-ordinating committee and, if agreement in principle was given, a sub-committee was charged with carrying out the detailed specification work. The detailed proposal was reported back to the co-ordinating committee for a final decision and recommendation to the board. Concerning the administrative systems, standard software packages had been bought in and any tailoring of the predominantly financial systems software was carried out by accountants with programming skills. Overall these arrangements could be described as a form of *de jure* tight control, based on a corporate philosophy that business needs should prevail and that computing facilities should be decentralised to user departments who would determine their requirements within that corporate framework.

With respect to the degree of centralisation of provision of computing facilities and expertise, these two cases display some sharp contrasts. Whereas the insurance firm was highly centralised both in terms of the provision of computer systems and the central pool of expertise to service users, the heating and ventilating firm had not only devolved its provision of computing facilities to user departments, but had also kept its central in-house specialists to a minimum and externalised other aspects of the servicing role. With reference to the degree of centralisation, the other four firms generally speaking occupy various positions between the two extremes outlined. The most ambiguous case is the electronics components manufacturer which provides an interesting illustration of the potential managerial problems posed by current developments in information technology.

Of the other four firms, the computer equipment manufacturer was the more decentralised in its provision of computing facilities and expertise. This was a large company with several sites in the UK and its head office was the subject of the study. Its central information systems department provided large-scale systems such as payroll and services such as office automation. Some head office departments had installed their own mainframe computers but these were run from the central computing department. Departments were relatively free to purchase microcomputers and software providing these complied with certain guidelines, particularly with regard to interfacing with the mainframe network. Thus regarding the provision of computing facilities this firm had struck a balance between centralisation and decentralisation, with the emphasis perhaps tending to the former. However, in relation to the provision of computing expertise it had adopted a much stronger policy of devolution.

The underlying theme of this policy of devolution was to encourage the development of skills so that departments could develop their own computer systems, without having to rely on central resources. Part of the reason for adopting the policy was the increasing demand from user departments for computing services, which could not easily be met centrally without large-scale recruitment and training. The policy adopted entailed setting up specialist groups within each user department, comprising staff redeployed from the central computing department and from the user department itself. Structures had also been established, in the form of steering committees and working groups, to co-ordinate the strategy for systems development and to share information and ideas, between similar user departments throughout the

93

whole company. These structures provided one element of the system of control over computerisation in this firm and, like the provision of expertise, this had been devolved to departments.

There was, however, a corporate framework of control comprising two main elements. The first element was the requirement for the devolved computing service groups to operate within the corporate planning process, to provide systems and services to support the needs of the business. The second element was the strong regulatory role that the central computing department played with respect to hardware, software and networking standards, in which it was increasingly playing a policing role. It was the custodian of company data, controlling and managing access to and use of those data. It also had a strong audit role, ensuring the adoption of good procedures and practices throughout the company. Finally, it was responsible for developing project disciplines, to ensure good project management which was flexible and avoided being over-bureaucratic.

The DIY firm was a fast-growing company with many retail outlets throughout the country and its head office was again the subject of the study. This firm had also decentralised certain aspects of its computing services, but not to the same extent as the computer manufacturer. Most of its large-scale systems, such as payroll and accounting, as well as its EPOS system, were centrally provided from its head office mainframe installation. A fairly large number of microcomputers were in use or planned to be introduced for a variety of uses. These uses ranged from the planned replacement of till controllers in the retail outlets by intelligent controllers, to a variety of dedicated tasks, systems development work and personal computing within head office. Networking was under active investigation.

At the time the study took place there was no direct access to the mainframe databases from microcomputers, although work was due to commence on the development of an on-line decision support system. Currently, therefore, microcomputer users had to rely on the central computing staff to facilitate the down-loading of mainframe data in a form suitable for their use on their own machines. Generally speaking, the provision of computing expertise was centralised, but regular monthly meetings of representatives from user departments were held to encourage the sharing of knowledge and experience. The central information services department had a responsibility for user support and this was encapsulated in a philosophy of encouraging end-user self-sufficiency.

Overall, decentralisation of computing services in this firm was still developing, although a fairly clear corporate strategy existed. Computer developments were co-ordinated and investment authorised through the finance director to whom the central computer department was responsible. The information services department had control over hardware and software standards and its approval was required for all procurement by user departments. The subsequent use of computer applications, particularly involving personal computing tools, was the responsibility of departmental line managers. The information services department was also developing control over company data, particularly through the establishment of carefully defined databases. Whilst the overall control over computerisation was relatively tight in this firm currently, this would obviously be put to the test should direct access to mainframe databases become available.

The pharmaceuticals firm was an American-owned company with three main sites in the UK, of which the largest (including its UK head office) was the subject of the study. This firm was an established user of computer systems and had a wide range of applications based on mainframe, minicomputer and microcomputer machines. The firm had a policy of integrating mainframe systems where practicable and there was also some interlinking of microcomputers into the mainframe systems. Computing expertise was centrally provided, including the provision of a service to microcomputer users. This service had been established in response to the proliferation of informal computing and the role was largely concerned with keeping up to date with the available software packages, so that users could be offered a range of options to suit their requirements. Overall, this firm had a computing service that was centralised to a similar degree to that found in the DIY firm.

Organisational control over computerisation in this firm was almost as tight as that in the heating and ventilating firm and perhaps even more formalised. As mentioned, a service had been established to provide advice to users on the availability of software packages. To that extent, decisions about computerisation were devolved to user departments. However, the purchase of all hardware and any major software developments had to be authorised, not only by the computer department, but also by the parent company in the USA. This meant that any department wanting to purchase even a single microcomputer had to obtain authorisation to do so, although the subsequent purchase of software packages was not so constrained.

Local decision-making about major hardware or software

developments was handled by a steering committee on computerisation, comprising senior company managers meeting quarterly. Development projects were initiated through the committee with implementation being devolved to a project team involving members of the user department and the computer department, but under the overall co-ordination of a member of the latter department. In summary, overall control over computerisation in this firm was fairly tight and formalised. Yet once authority was received to acquire microcomputing hardware, user departments had a relatively free hand to develop their informal computing provided this did not require too much development work.

The electronics components manufacturer was the most ambiguous case and it is worth comparing it with the pharmaceuticals firm to highlight the more interesting features. This firm was part of a multinational electrical and electronics company. It had been using computer systems for many years and had a similarly diverse range of applications based on a variety of hardware located in different departments. In one sense this firm might be considered to be relatively decentralised with regard to its provision of computing facilities. However, unlike the pharmaceuticals firm, this was a very fragmented form of decentralisation generally characterised by duplication of data and incompatibility of systems.

Thus there was a lack of integration of computing facilities and the difficulty of pursuing integration was compounded by the question of departmental 'ownership' of their own hardware. The main area where there was some integration was in relation to administrative systems linked to the London-based head office of the firm's parent company. Concerning the second organisational variable, overall organisational control was relatively loose, particularly with regard to the separate departmental facilities. Although there was a representative inter-departmental committee dealing with electronic communications and networks, as well as general policy documents from the parent company, there was no overall policy for either systems integration or data transferability. Whilst the regulation of administrative systems was tighter, there were difficulties in extending that influence due to the issues of ownership and systems incompatibility.

Overall, this firm could be seen to be characterised by incompatible forms of centralisation and decentralisation of its computing service provision. The strategy which it was seeking to develop was based on the need for an information policy, rather than a computerisation policy as such. The main ingredients of this developing information policy were basically threefold. The first element was the need to ensure that data requirements were defined by the manufacturing system, so that integration could be oriented to production needs rather than towards functional elegance. The second element was the creation of organisational arrangements which would enable expertise to be shared without the frictions associated with ownership. The third element was the need to get senior managers to agree a framework for achieving the other two objectives. Thus what might be described as the need for a corporate framework of control could be seen as the key to the managerial dilemma for this firm.

CONCLUSIONS

The aim of this chapter was to report some empirical findings illustrating the kinds of responses being made to the current dilemma of managing computing facilities. The source of the dilemma was identified as arising from technological developments which can simultaneously facilitate centralisation and decentralisation. The substance of the dilemma was described as a search for organisational forms which strike a balance between the maintenance of centralised control and the provision of decentralised facilities. The findings were discussed with reference to two organisational variables which, it was suggested, should be jointly considered by managers seeking to construct organisational forms for flexible computing. These organisational variables were, firstly, the degree of central or devolved provision of computing facilities and computing expertise and, secondly, but crucially, the extent and manner of control over computer developments and standards. The findings suggest several points worthy of consideration.

It was implicit in the cases described that the stage of computerisation reached and, in particular, the circumstances leading to it, were an important factor in a firm's present strategy. Other factors, such as the complexity and stability of the task environment, the diversity and scale of applications extant within an organisation, together with the degree of integrative potential or compatibility of systems, will have a significant bearing on the acuteness of the managerial dilemma. Whilst these factors will not dictate either centralised or decentralised provision of computing facilities and expertise, they will affect the strategy that can be adopted towards shifting the balance one way or the other.

Technically speaking, it is clear that there are few constraints on the form of provision of computing facilities or the amount of integration achievable. It would seem that the crucial issues are the way in which expertise is provided to support that provision of facilities and the system of control that is adopted to regulate it. Limitations of space mean that it is not possible to explore the implications of the politics of organisations here. Clearly, that is an area which needs investigation if the outcomes of the centralisation versus decentralisation debate within organisations are to be properly understood.

REFERENCES

Child, J. (1984) 'New Technology and Developments in Management Organisation', *Omega*, 12, 3, pp. 211–23

King, J.L. (1983) 'Centralised versus Decentralised Computing: Organisational Considerations and Management Options', *Computing Surveys*, 15, 4, pp. 319–49

Leavitt, H.J. and Whisler, T.H. (1958) 'Management in the 1980s', *Harvard Business Review*, 36, pp. 41–8

Peters, T.J. and Waterman, R.H. (1982) *In Search of Excellence: Lessons from America's Best-run Companies*, Harper & Row, New York

Robey, D. (1977) 'Computers and Management Structure: Some Empirical Findings Re-examined', *Human Relations*, 30, 11, pp. 963–75

——— (1981) 'Computer Information Systems and Organisation Structure', *Communications of the ACM*, 24, 10, pp. 679–87

——— (1983) 'Information Systems and Organisational Change: A Comparative Case Study', *Systems, Objectives, Solutions*, 3, pp. 143–54

Webb, T. (1985) 'Towards More Flexible Computing?', *Management Services*, September, pp. 16–19

9

Organisational Choice in the Redesign of Supervisory Systems

Patrick Dawson and Ian McLoughlin

INTRODUCTION

Supervisors have long been regarded as a problem by organisational practitioners in the UK (see Dawson, 1986a, pp. 13–36). Child and Partridge (1982) argue that supervisors have become 'lost managers', who, instead of being able to set the parameters and targets within which they work, now have these set by functional specialists and senior managers. This is experienced as an erosion of their authority by supervisors, which in turn reflects on their ability to execute their responsibilities. The situation is compounded by the supervisor's loss of status in the eyes of management. This is symbolised for Child and Partridge by an account of the visit by a group personnel director of a large engineering company to one of its Midlands plants. After the visit an instruction was issued that supervisors should no longer drink tea from cups and saucers but use the vending machines like their subordinates. A week later all the supervisors had joined a trade union and submitted a claim for more pay (1982, p. 11).

It has been suggested that the problematic status of supervision is exacerbated by the introduction of new computer-based information technologies (Buchanan and Boddy, 1983). One argument has been that the new technology erodes the role of the supervisor by making it possible to centralise control in the hands of higher levels of management (Edwards, 1979). An alternative view is that technological change enables a move from traditional supervisory concerns with the direct control of labour to a role which requires supervisors to be retrained as technical experts (Woodward, 1980). Our research over the past five years goes some way to support Child and Partridge's 'lost managers' thesis. However, we have observed the emergence of a new type of supervisory role based around the task of information management.

We will illustrate in this chapter how the adoption of new computer-based technologies can lead to an erosion of supervisory roles in at least three ways. First, changes in the skill requirement of operating staff can lead to an emergent 'skill superiority' of operatives and work groups over their immediate supervisors. Second, the emergence of new roles to accomplish operational control tasks connected with management's use of the new technology can lead to conflicts between 'new' and 'old' types of supervisory roles. Third, changes in supervisory systems may have broader implications for management organisation as elements of existing organisational structures become redundant.

It is our view, however, that the erosion of supervisory roles is not an unavoidable 'impact' of computer technology. Rather, we would argue that it reflects a failure on the part of organisational practitioners to come to terms with the problems and opportunities which the new technology brings. Our research has also shown that these problems are rarely anticipated or fully understood by either management or unions representing supervisors, when new technology is introduced. Consequently, existing problems relating to supervision tend to be highlighted, and attempts to resolve the situation are often hampered by traditional management thinking (see also Buchanan, 1983). In particular, the issue of supervisory training is often overlooked during the implementation and initial operation of new computer-based technologies (Rothwell and Davidson, 1983).

We intend illustrating the need for organisational practitioners to tackle these problems by discussing empirical examples drawn from a series of case studies in which the authors have been involved. These studies concern: telephone exchange modernisation in British Telecom; the introduction of CAD in engineering drawing offices; and the introduction of a computer information system in British Rail.[1]

One difficulty in discussions of supervision is the failure in much of the literature to define adequately the nature of the roles being referred to. The tendency has been to assume that supervision centres on the task of labour control at the workplace, and that supervisors can be identified by job titles. In practice, however, the job of the supervisor often embraces a far broader range of 'operational control' tasks which may be performed by individuals who are not formally defined as 'supervisors' (Dawson and McLoughlin,

1986; Thurley and Hamblin, 1964). Following Thurley and Wirdenius (1973), we have adopted the concept of 'supervisory system' to refer to the network of formally and informally recognised and interrelated roles which are concerned with the direct day-to-day control of production or service operations (Dawson and McLoughlin, 1986, pp. 118–19). The main point to bear in mind for the following discussion is that the implications of information technology for supervision do not just concern the traditional labour control responsibilities of the formally defined foreman or first line supervisor. Rather, they extend to a wider set of organisational roles which may not have supervisory job titles, and yet are an integral part of workplace supervisory systems of control. Accordingly, the organisational choices open to management in redesigning supervisory roles in the context of technological change are far broader than might otherwise be assumed (Dawson and McLoughlin, 1986, p. 129).

THE PROBLEM OF 'SKILL SUPERIORITY'

The phenomenon of 'skill superiority' is reasonably well documented in studies of the implications of computer-based technologies (Buchanan and Boddy, 1983, p. 249). The introduction of computer systems, and the retraining of operatives in their utilisation, has resulted in the deskilling of supervisors who are no longer knowledgeable about the work being done by their subordinates. In our experience, the significance of this erosion lies not so much in the reduction of control responsibility of the supervisor, but in the erosion of an important symbol of their authority over subordinates, namely, their extensive experience and knowledge of the work they are supervising. While supervisors frequently retain control responsibilities when new technology is introduced, they are rarely equipped with the necessary skills in the form of adequate or appropriate retraining which will enable them to execute these responsibilities. In other words, the mismatch between responsibility and authority identified by Child and Partridge (1982) may be further highlighted by the introduction of new technology.

An excellent example of this is provided by a study of the introduction of new telephone exchange technologies in British Telecom (BT) (Clark et al., 1987). Here a new semi-electronic exchange system was introduced to replace an electro-mechanical system which had been in use by BT since the 1920s. The new

101

technology required a new electronics based 'systems oriented' set of mental skills on the part of the technicians who had to maintain the exchanges. The old exchange technology required electro-mechanical skills with the emphasis on manual dexterities. Traditionally, maintenance supervisors were promoted from the ranks of maintenance technicians after several years of service and had an intimate knowledge of the jobs of their subordinates. Whilst in practice the maintenance technicians enjoyed considerable individual autonomy in the execution of their work, the 'skill superiority' of the supervisors did provide an important symbol of their authority to intervene in day-to-day work operations when an operational contingency, such as a major exchange fault, occurred.

The introduction of the new technology transformed this situation. The supervisors were provided with a brief, two-week appreciation course on the maintenance of the new exchange system, a situation seen as perfectly adequate by both management and the supervisors' union. The technicians' courses lasted 17 weeks. Once their exchanges were operational, the maintenance technicians quickly developed a 'skill superiority' in relation to their supervisors. The role of the supervisor, already marginal under the old technology, became almost redundant as far as the maintenance technicians were concerned. This was reflected in the experience of the supervisors themselves, who in the absence of any managerial guidance on how to supervise maintenance in the new exchanges, tended to withdraw completely from any day-to-day operational control responsibilities. As one commented:

> I've only got the sketchiest outline of the technology. I can't make a useful engineering contribution. If you've got 'troubles' (i.e. a technical problem) you feel much happier if you know what you are talking about. I am now purely a paper engineer. On the old exchange system I definitely influenced the actions taken by the technicians. I could look at a problem and say 'take that course of action' and I knew that if it was done properly it would work. Now I can't say that (quoted in Clark *et al.*, 1987).

THE PROBLEM OF OLD AND NEW SUPERVISORY ROLES

When new systems are introduced it has frequently been noted that new managerial and supervisory roles are created in relation to the new technology. The most dramatic example of this is probably the emergence of data processing departments with the introduction of large mainframe installations for batch processing tasks. The more recent introduction of computer-based information technology seems to have involved less large-scale changes in organisational arrangements, but nevertheless new roles and positions have emerged. Buchanan and Boddy report from a broad range of studies that, in most cases, organisation structures were ramified by the creation of new specialist groups, new management hierarchies and new positions (1983, p. 245). They note that one effect of this was to take operating control responsibility away from operatives, which tended to interfere with their ability to use the technology effectively. Our research suggests that an additional problem occurs in the relationship between the 'new' supervisory roles created as a result of the introduction of new systems, and the existing supervisory arrangements.

An example of this is provided in a study by one of the authors of the introduction of computer aided drafting/design (CAD) technology in engineering drawing offices (McLoughlin, 1987). When introducing CAD systems management have various choices in the way they can organise work around the technology. Broadly speaking these choices involve decisions on whether to:

1. Locate CAD workstations in a central 'CAD Centre', or to locate them amongst conventional drawing boards in existing offices.
2. Allocate each CAD workstation to a dedicated 'CAD operator' — a specially selected draftsperson retrained to use the new technology — or to adopt a non-dedicated operator approach where all drafting staff are retrained and can 'book' time to use a CAD workstation.

In the British engineering industry the drawing office union TASS has a national policy which seeks retraining in the new technology for all its members. Normally it appears to be the case that firms adopting CAD agree to this condition, but at the same time insist on locating their CAD workstations in a CAD Centre under the control of a 'CAD manager'.

This was precisely the arrangement at a shipbuilding firm visited by one of the authors. The firm had three conventional drawing offices employing over 100 drafting staff. Staff were divided into groups under the supervision of section leaders, themselves experienced draftspeople. A 30 workstation CAD system had been installed and was located in two separate purpose-built offices adjacent to the three conventional drawing offices. In accordance with an agreement with TASS, all drawing office staff were retrained. They received a five-week training course, and the section leaders an eight-day 'appreciation course'. The result was the same as in the British Telecom case, an emergent skill superiority of the drafting staff over their section leaders. However, in this case the problem was compounded by the new role of the CAD manager.

The CAD manager had no formal responsibility for drafting staff but was responsible for the provision and administration of the CAD facility as a service to the drawing offices, including training and technical support. Each week the section leaders were responsible for bidding for time for their staff on the CAD workstations. The CAD manager allocated workstations to staff, and adjudicated where demands clashed or priority work had to be accomplished. The CAD manager believed the attitude of section leaders was crucial in the successful utilisation of the system, since it was they who made decisions over whether drawings were to be made conventionally or using CAD. In practice, problems occurred with some section leaders who felt the CAD manager was subverting their role. The CAD manager admitted that in practice drafting staff now tended to seek technical advice from him, rather then their section leaders, when using the system. The section leaders felt the CAD workstations should have been located in the drawing offices where they could more directly supervise their staff.

THE PROBLEM OF REDUNDANT SUPERVISORY ROLES

Child (1984) suggests that information technologies offer a means of increasing management control by integrating the direct day-to-day control of production operations with strategic operating objectives. This is made possible by the provision of faster and more precise knowledge about operating conditions, a reduction in the scope for indeterminacy in the behaviour of employees, and the unification of previously segmented control systems (1984, p. 258). One widely predicted organisational consequence of the adoption of information technology has been a rapid slimming down of redundant elements of supervisory systems such as middle management and associated clerical staff previously responsible for the capture, analysis and communication of information. This results in a move from rigid hierarchical structures to more flexible organisational forms (Rose, 1969; Child, 1984, p. 260).

Whilst such moves towards integration of operational and strategic elements in supervisory systems may now be possible technically, it appears that in practice organisational integration is much harder to achieve. Our last empirical example provides an instance of this. The case in question was a study by the authors of a mainframe computer information system used by British Rail to control its freight operations (Dawson and McLoughlin, 1986; Dawson, 1986b). The system was introduced by British Rail in the early 1970s to combat major operational control problems in keeping track of freight wagons and locomotives. Prior to computerisation, information on the whereabouts of wagons and locomotives was collected in local marshalling yards and freight terminals by supervisors and communicated to one of 20 or so Divisional Control Offices which covered the national rail network. The first hour of the supervisor's working day was often occupied ensuring that a physical check had been made on the stock of wagons in the yard, and then telephoning the details to Divisional Control. These local reports were collated by Divisional Controllers who would attempt to produce a 'picture' of the current state of freight operations under their jurisdiction. This information would then be transmitted to one of five Regional Control Officers who would control and co-ordinate the inter-regional movements of freight train services. At national level an attempt was made to monitor the movements of freight over the entire rail network. However, most day-to-day operating decisions involving the running and cancellation of freight services were taken at Divisional level.

The collection, collation, interpretation and dissemination of this information from local to national level, and then the transmission of decisions affecting the movements of freight, could take up to ten hours. Moreover, there was no way of validating the reports received and hence the accuracy of this information was open to question. Thus a situation existed where management's attempt to control operations were retrospective and largely ineffective, with the result that local supervisors were not fully integrated into the wider system of management control. This was reflected in the parochial attitude of supervisors who would have recourse to informal methods and rules of thumb in order to acquire the necessary wagon stock to meet local fluctuations in the volume of freight and changing customer demands. In particular, it was common practice for supervisors to hoard wagons and locomotives to make sure they had sufficient resources to meet their requirements.

Computer technology has been used by management to provide

accurate 'real-time' information of the location and status of British Rail wagons and locomotives over the whole rail freight network. Management's strategy in exploiting the enabling characteristics of the computer technology involved a reorganisation of its system for controlling freight operations. The new information flows and communication channels provided by the computer obviated the need for a hierarchical reporting structure. Information about operating conditions and performance at remote locations was now immediately available to headquarters management. Moreover, access to the real-time database maintained by the computer was also available at local level. This meant that much of the decision-making responsibility exercised at divisional level for local freight operations could be delegated to the point at which the operations occurred. In order to achieve this objective 152 computer reporting centres linked by terminals to the mainframe computers were located in and around marshalling yards to receive reports from guards, shunters and supervisors which could then be transmitted to the central computer. In order to exploit this new computer-generated information a new supervisory role was designed. This role was defined as a second-line or senior supervisory post, and was given formal responsibility for the control of area operations. The primary task centred on utilising the information transmitted to the various reporting centres in making 'real-time' operating decisions on the running, cancellation and alteration of freight train services. This enabled both an extension of the range of decisions made about day-to-day operations at local level and a widening of the geographical span of supervisory control to cover all operations in a defined responsibility area around each of the marshalling yards.

In theory this new computer-based information flow made the intermediate level of the old reporting structure redundant. However, at the time of implementing the system management had no plans to scrap the role of Divisional Controls. Moreover, subsequent management plans to completely decentralise operational control responsibility to the local level were frustrated by trade union and middle management resistance to the abolition of Divisional Controls. This would have involved the loss of around 1,000 supervisory posts and would have meant the destruction of a traditional element of the railway operating structure which had an important status in the organisation's culture. Indeed, in the face of this resistance, it was only some ten years later that significant changes began to be made in the Divisional Control structure, and then only on a region-by-region basis. Thus at the time of our research we observed the anomalous situation of one supervisory system, focused around a new computer-based role, existing alongside the remnants of the 'old' supervisory system previously focused on the Divisional Control offices. Formally the new supervisors were meant to work closely with their Divisional Control offices, but in practice they worked largely independently of them. Despite the fact that the persistence of some elements of the old supervisory system was seen by many freight managers as a 'barrier' to the full exploitation of the new technology, they appeared reluctant to embark on any radical organisational innovation in the wake of technological change. Rather, they were content to allow the old system to 'wither on the vine' as the extent of its redundance became apparent.

CONCLUSION: ENTER THE INFORMATION MANAGER?

According to Child and Partridge (1982, pp. 206–18), there are four possible options open to organisational practitioners in the redesign of supervisory roles. First, to abolish the role of the supervisor through delegating routine supervisory tasks to workgroup leaders (1982, p. 206). Second, to leave the role as it is, but make improvements through clarifying the distinction between managerial and supervisory roles (1982, p. 208). Third, to develop supervision into a genuine first-line managerial role (1982, p. 210). Fourth, to develop the role into a purely technical function (1982, p. 213). We would argue that the definition of these problems is based on a narrow definition of supervision, and that the options open to organisational practitioners are in fact far broader than Child and Partridge (1982) suggest. In our view, the introduction of computer-based systems presents the opportunity to redesign a range of roles within supervisory systems around the task of information management. This task is concerned directly with exploiting the capabilities of the technology to provide 'real-time' information on the status and performance of work operations.

We believe that each of the cases discussed above presents, in embryonic form at least, the basis for such new supervisory roles of information management. This is probably most developed in the case of TOPS in British Rail, where the nature of the technology concerned resulted in new flows of real-time information on the status of freight operations. In this instance, as we saw, management decided to create a new type of managerial/supervisory position to exploit the operations control potential of the new technology. This, we would suggest, is a blueprint for the kind of 'information manager' role we have in mind, where the receipt, analysis and manipulation of information on operating conditions and performance in order to make operational decisions are the core features of the new supervisory roles emerging in organisation using computer-based technologies.

This development is also apparent in relation to CAD. In particular, the case in question concerns an organisation seeking to move towards a computer-integrated manufacturing system. Here the CAD system was used to construct a database from which production information could be extracted and supplied in tightly specified forms to the shipyard. It was readily apparent that, as the system was developed, the CAD manager would assume an increasingly important role as manager of this information database. In the British Telecom case, the type of semi-electronic exchange system being introduced was having various computer systems attached to it to aid the monitoring of performance and identify maintenance priorities. In the new fully electronic systems about to be introduced this kind of computer-aided maintenance management is fully incorporated within the system. Both these developments provide the basis for a new information management role for maintenance supervisors (Clark *et al.*, 1987).

However, it was quite clear in all three cases that the new opportunities being presented by computer-based systems were only gradually being realised and developed, and that constraints on this process existed. In the case of BR considerable uncertainty surrounded the nature of the role of the new supervisor on the part of local managers. The supervisors themselves felt local management did not understand their role and argued that they should be a management grade. Significantly, whilst little of their job involved the direct control of labour, the supervisors still received general training in labour supervision as well as information management training. In the case of the general adoption of CAD, significant constraints would appear to exist on the development of the information manager role in so far as many firms are using the technology purely as an 'electronic drawing board', rather than as a means for constructing a common information database to integrate design and manufacture. The BT case indicated that the development of the information manager role may involve the delegation of some day-to-day supervisory responsibility to the work group itself in organising and executing work tasks. Such a change would raise considerable industrial relations difficulties for both management and unions.

The number of options open to organisational practitioners in the development of supervision extend beyond those associated with the conventional labour-management functions of traditional supervisory roles. We have shown how the utilisation of computers in the control of workplace operations is becoming an additional supervisory task integral to the function of workplace operations management. The three case studies reported illustrate a range of differing problems which may arise in the development and redesign of supervisory systems around new computer-based technology. In particular, these studies have shown how both management and unions often neglect the importance of developing suitable training courses to meet the changing skill requirements of supervisors, and how they rarely ensure the integration of supervisory roles into management structures. Moreover, we would argue that the need for practitioners to seriously consider the problems of organisational choice in the redesign of supervisory systems is further highlighted by the apparent potential for a new type of information manager role. However, it is essential that an evaluation of the options is undertaken during the implementation of new technology and not belatedly, after it has been introduced. We therefore conclude by stressing the need for a more proactive strategy towards supervision, and would further suggest that such a course of action may in itself demonstrate how the so-called 'problem' of supervision does not stem from 'the supervisor' but, rather, from a misunderstanding of the potential for supervisory development on the part of organisational practitioners.

NOTE AND REFERENCES

1. The British Rail and British Telecom study formed part of a programme of research conducted by the New Technology Research Group at Southampton University, and was funded by the SERC/ESRC Joint Committee. The CAD case studies were funded by the ESRC under a Post-Doctoral Fellowship scheme, and were hosted by the Department of Sociology and Social Administration at Southampton University.

Buchanan, D. (1983) 'Technological Imperatives and Strategic Choice', in G. Winch (ed.), *Information Technology in Manufacturing Processes*, Rossendale
——— and Boddy, D. (1983) *Organisations in the Computer Age: Technological Imperatives and Strategic Choice*, Gower, Aldershot

Child, J. (1984) *Organisation: A Guide to Problems and Practice*, 2nd edn, Harper & Row, New York
——— and Partridge, B. (1982) *Lost Managers: Supervisors in Industry and Society*, Cambridge University Press, Cambridge
Clark, J., McLoughlin, I., Rose, H. and King, R. (1987) *Technological Change in the Workplace*, Cambridge University Press, Cambridge
Dawson, P.M.B. (1986a) *Computer Technology and the Redefinition of Supervision*, Ph.D. thesis, University of Southampton
——— (1986b) 'How Computers Affect Supervisory Systems of Control', in A. Roff and D. Brown (eds), *Business Case File in Information Technology*, Van Nostrand Reinhold, New York
——— (1987) 'Computer Technology and the Job of the First-Line Supervisor', *New Technology, Work and Employment*, 2, 1
——— and McLoughlin, I.P. (1986) 'Computer Technology and the Redefinition of Supervision: A Study of the Effects of Computerisation on Railway Freight Supervisors', *Journal of Management Studies*, 23, 1
Edwards, R. (1979) *Contested Terrain: The Transformation of the Workplace in the Twentieth Century*, Heinemann, London
McLoughlin, I.P. (1987) 'Management Strategies for the Introduction and Control of Interactive Computer Graphics Systems', in the proceedings of the workshop on *Social Science Studies on CAD/CAM in Europe*, Kernforschungszentrum, Karlsruhe
Rose, M. (1969) *Computers, Management and Society*, Penguin, Harmondsworth
Rothwell, S. and Davidson, D. (1983) 'Training for New Technology', in G. Winch (ed), *Information Technology in Manufacturing Processes*, Rossendale, London
Thurley, K.E. and Hamblin, A.C. (1964) 'The Supervisor and His Job', *Problems of Progress in Industry*, no 13, HMSO, London
Thurley, K.E. and Wirdenius, H. (1973) *Supervision: A Reappraisal*, Heinemann, London
Woodward, J. (1980) *Industrial Organization: Theory and Practice*, 2nd edn, Oxford University Press, London

10

New Techniques for Recording Time at Work: Their Implications for Supervisory Training and Development

Nicholas Kinnie and Alan Arthurs

INTRODUCTION

Time recording devices have been used in industry for more than a hundred years. They are traditionally associated with 'clocking-in' and 'clocking-out', where the arrival and departure of a worker is recorded by a time clock. The records are used primarily for payment and disciplinary purposes. New, computer-based systems have been available for several years. They can be an integral part of a wider management information system, permitting factory-wide collection of data, automatic analysis and selective control of access to buildings.

In this chapter we discuss some of the results of a project which examines the introduction of these computerised techniques into industrial time recording. We look at the changes in supervisory roles associated with the introduction of MTR (mechanised time recording) and their training and development implications. The term 'supervisor' refers to the first line of management, and will be known alternatively as foreman or section leader in some organisations. Our research was conducted in late 1985 and early 1986, during which time we investigated five companies' decisions to develop computer-based time recording. Table 10.1 gives some brief details of the cases studied.

These computer-based systems are marketed as having overwhelming advantages over the older electro-mechanical time recorders. They can provide instant data about an employee's attendance at a particular work station. This information can be transmitted to the production controller, who can then make decisions about manning levels and the mobility of labour. Aggregated data can be used to identify patterns of lateness and absence, and to

Table 10.1: Industrial time recorders — the cases studied

Name	Employees	Activity	MTR introduced	Type of MTR Basic	Payroll	MIS
Components	1,500	Production line	1977	x	x	x
Consumer Products	750	Mass production	1982	x	x	x
Luxury Goods	1,650	Manufacture of components	1984	x	x	x Limited
Assembly	5,000	Production line assembly	1981	x	x	x Limited
Hightech	8,000	Manufacture and assembly of components	1984	x	x	

Notes: Basic — microprocessor-based replacements for time clocks.
Payroll — direct link between data collection terminals and payroll files.
MIS — Management information systems providing aggregated daily and weekly reports.

supply information on overtime and allocation of labour costs. The costs of running the timekeeping system can be reduced by the automatic preparation of time cards — wage calculations are simplified by the automatic totalling of hours. Opportunities for the card-handling abuses associated with traditional clocking are reduced, particularly where an employee's security pass and time card are combined (Kinnie and Arthurs, 1986).

NEW TECHNOLOGY AND SUPERVISORS

Some studies have argued that new technology provides the opportunity to decentralise control and strengthen the authority of supervisors (Davis and Taylor, 1976; Woodward, 1980). Others suggest that technical change weakens supervisory authority, undermining their responsibilities by introducing machine pacing of operatives, automatic analysis of production performance information and giving more autonomy to operators (Child and Partridge, 1982; Leavitt and Whisler, 1958). Finally, there are those who argue that computerisation permits both greater control from senior managers and at the same time an enhanced role for those with supervisory responsibilities (Dawson and McLoughlin, 1986).

We argue that supervisors' jobs change in different ways; in some cases their authority is strengthened, while in others it is weakened. It is the variety rather than consistency of experience observed which is most noticeable in the companies studied. These variations are traced back to the strategic decisions managers make in the choice, implementation and operation of the technology employed.

We find unhelpful a model of change which assumes that management chooses the most suitable technology, which then requires organisational adjustments in order to maximise efficiency (Senker, 1985, p. 2). A more attractive model is one which sees technology as sufficiently flexible and malleable to fit any one of a number of managerial objectives. Clearly, the setting of these managerial objectives is a political process (Bessant, 1983; Buchanan and Boddy, 1983; Child 1972; Wilkinson, 1983). Managers can influence the technology at the time of its design, its choice and during its implementation and debugging (Wilkinson, 1983, pp. 86–92). At each of these stages the politics of decision-making will influence the changes taking place; the use and design of training programmes are part of this political process.

CHANGING SUPERVISORY ROLES

Three changes in supervisory roles associated with MTR are examined in this section, First, the changes in the executive or decision-making role made possible by improved management information systems. Second, the alterations in the supervisory role resulting from the changed time recording arrangements. Finally, the modifications to the disciplinary role of supervisors emanating from new procedures for penalising punctuality and rewarding good attendance. Each of these roles is surrounded by a set of customs and practices which are often unique to that supervisor and highly resistant to change. Particular attention will be given to the discretion enjoyed by supervisors before and after the introduction of the new techniques.

Executive role

Supervisors play a major role in the day-to-day organisation and control of work. They are involved in making a multiplicity of decisions aimed at achieving targets on time and at the right cost and quality. The more advanced MTR systems are designed to change the way supervisors take manning level decisions. For example in 'Luxury Goods' these devices were installed to replace a traditional clock card system to give accurate and up-to-date figures on attendance compared with the number required to operate. Manning level decisions in this case were central to maintaining production because the mix of skills was critical and a prompt start to production was seen as vital. The intention was that the new MTR system would improve the quality of decision-making through having more accurate information more quickly, particularly in highly dispersed sections.

This change could potentially affect supervisory discretion in two ways. First, there could be a strengthening of discretion since supervisors had more information more quickly and so were in a better position to make manning decisions. Second, supervisory discretion could be weakened since information on attendance, previously available only to them, was now available to their bosses as well.

In practice, however, neither of these possibilities was fully realised since supervisors were disinclined to make full use of the system because of what they claimed were technical and access problems. The new system was slow to collect the information and had a relatively long response time. Not all supervisors had immediate access to a VDU because of a shortage of screens. The result was that supervisors tended to fall back on their established practice of making manning level decisions on the basis of the 'rule of thumb'. Typically this involved moving men around and borrowing from other supervisors in order to get the line started, and then looking for permanent replacements once work was underway.

Managers did not tend to usurp the authority of their subordinates for three reasons. First, there was the view expressed by one manager that manning level decisions were the responsibility of the supervisor and 'why should we reduce the manager to the level of the foreman?' Second, there were occasions when the managers were not inclined to use the system because they had doubts about its value. Finally, the delay in receiving information which inhibited the supervisors also prevented managers from intervening even if they wanted to.

Supervisory role

A key role of the supervisor is to exercise control over employees and materials in order to achieve his or her objectives. Typically a whole series of informal customs will be developed relating to the control of overtime and the allocation of jobs.

Three different experiences were observed when studying changes in the supervisory role. First, supervisory authority was reduced in 'Assembly' with the introduction of a new system to control the amount of overtime worked. Under the old system the amount of overtime actually worked in a section could be 'hidden' from management. However, a new MTR system meant that overtime figures were collected automatically from clockings and relayed to management. Under the new system supervisors had much less room to manoeuvre, as monitoring by their supervisors became tighter.

In 'Consumer Products' supervisory authority was greatly enhanced by the new MTR system which coincided with a move to a group-based production system. The old production line technology was replaced by a number of groups each responsible for the whole product. Supervisors became group leaders who were now responsible for forward loading as well as the normal supervisory duties which they had performed previously. The information supplied by the MTR system was vital in supporting their new role of managing the whole of the group activity.

Finally, in 'Components' supervisors' authority was strengthened but at the same time they were also made more responsible for their subordinates. Supervisors' discretion was increased since they were able to input directly into attendance and payroll files to resolve any employee queries over wages and other entitlements. Under the old system this was in the hands of the now defunct payroll department. The MTR system also required supervisors to resolve any 'mismatches' between the number of employees planned to be on their section and the number actually in attendance. This replaced the manual system of 'crewsheets' which supervisors filled in every day to account for the number of employees on their section. A monitoring device built into the system meant these mismatches could no longer be ignored, whereas previously, as one manager put it, 'all the information was on ''bits of paper'' and supervisors could hide behind the inefficiency of the system'.

Disciplinary role

Supervisors play a key role in enforcing company procedures and rules through the exercise of discipline. Customs and practices frequently spring up over lateness and early leaving, particularly in the way timekeeping offenders are treated. The disciplinary role of supervisors under MTR systems varied in two principal ways. There were those systems where supervisors became more removed from the process of disciplining employees for lateness and early leaving, while in other systems they assumed much greater responsibility.

In 'Assembly' managers sought to wrest the timekeeping disciplinary function away from the supervisor. Principally this involved removing supervisory discretion by paying employees to the minute automatically, and by paying a fixed weekly attendance supplement to employees with a perfect timekeeping record. Under the old system using clock cards employees would be 'quartered' if they arrived after the period of grace allowed, normally three minutes. Supervisors had the opportunity to sign the card to prevent an employee losing pay if it was thought that the reason given for lateness was adequate. The logic of the new system was that it would allow supervisors to concentrate on other issues such as job control and employee motivation which were seen as fundamental to efficiency.

An alternative view taken by senior managers in 'Hightech' was that a weakening of supervisory authority over timekeeping would undermine their credibility on a much wider range of issues. Consequently they maintained the position of supervisors in the centre of timekeeping discipline by allowing them to input directly into the system. Supervisors were permitted to create clockings, after consultation with employees, if, for example, someone had genuinely forgotten to clock in. This coincided with the introduction of supervisory log books designed to prevent supervisors relying on the MTR system as a 'prop'. Supervisors were encouraged to record any persistent pattern of lateness or absenteeism by their subordinates. Referred to by one manager as the supervisors' 'black book', these records were intended to be kept for both manual and staff workers so that timekeeping would become a 'tighter ship'. Previously, persistent offenders could slip through the net because supervisors did not keep individual records. Supervisors were encouraged to do this because they knew that the MTR records were available to their bosses who were looking for a reduction in total lost time. However, a number of supervisors were at pains to point out the data produced was only the base line, 'the figures don't tell you why a man is absent and how to get him back to work'.

PROBLEMS ASSOCIATED WITH SUPERVISORY TRAINING AND DEVELOPMENT

Several studies have looked at ways managers might cope with the training and development needs of supervisors following changes in technology. This section looks at some of these proposals and considers the obstacles in their path.

Some authors have recommended that managers ought to adopt a 'strategic approach' to planning for technical change. Part of this approach should ensure 'that the workforce can be trained to operate and maintain new systems' (Senker, 1985, p. 2). To do this managers must anticipate the training needs ahead of or in parallel with the innovation cycle, rather than being 'plugged in' after the change. Here the trainer's job is to act as 'a predictor and catalyst ensuring that the skills, knowledge, and attitudes the company needs now and the different ones they may need in the future are recognised and developed' (Walters, 1983, p. 206).

Managerial practice, however, as observed in the cases studied, appears to be rather different. Supervisors were not consulted before the changes, received little in the way of training, and did not always change their behaviour in the way intended following the training.

Ignorance of time recording practices

Within the management hierarchy supervisors, as distinct from production management, were commonly politically weak. Consequently, here as elsewhere, low priority was attached to the views and needs of supervisors and trainers because of 'urgent technical and operating pressures experienced by organisations unused to coping with such complexity' (Rothwell and Davidson, 1983, p. 124).

Lacking political muscle, supervisors were generally not consulted during the design or commissioning phase in any of the cases. Because their jobs were not affected directly supervisors were often thought of after rather than before the change. Supervisors were not consulted by management not simply because they were politically weak but also because of the ambiguity surrounding their role. The strategic model put forward suggests that the change programme should involve assessing current supervisory activity and a review of possible alternatives. However, special problems exist when carrying out this kind of analysis because 'there is almost inevitably an inconsistency between the supervisor's "perceived" role (as he sees it), his manifest role (what activity analysis shows he actually does with his time) and the "expected role" (what his superiors expect him to do)' (Dunkerley, 1975, p. 145).

The implications of this lack of consultation are profound, however, since the nature of technical change is more of a tactical than a strategic problem. The success of technical changes will be influenced by the extent to which they 'fit with existing pattern of production, local tradition of innovation, and previous success or failure with innovation, industrial relations, workforce attitudes and so on' (Bessant, 1983, pp.15–16). Thus the burden for achieving change falls more on the shoulders of managers and supervisors than on those at board level who make the strategic decisions.

Senior managers' lack of consultation with supervisors created several problems in the strategic decision-making process since they are unaware of the whole multitude of customs and practices which grow up on the shop floor which are known only to individual supervisors. Indeed, in 'Luxury Goods' there was no one who knew all of their informal time recording practices. This ignorance meant that senior managers were unsure what they were changing from and what they wanted to move towards. In the words of one manager in 'Luxury Goods', 'it was very difficult for us to specify to the software house what we wanted because we didn't know ourselves'. Often a process of trial and error has to be used, with the system being modified as it is put into operation. There was also the problem of managers' ignorance of what was available leading to missed opportunities to integrate information systems. In 'Assembly' there were two parallel, but quite separate, programmes for the computerisation of personnel records and the mechanisation of time recording.

Supervisors might also fall foul of the politics of technical change. In 'Hightech' there were two competing techniques put forward to mechanise time recording, each of which had very different implications for the supervisor. One, supported by the Finance department, was designed to provide quick and accurate collection of data for payroll purposes. The second, supported by the Production department, concentrated on the collection of a wide range of shop floor data of which attendance data were just one part. Something of a power struggle was taking place here to the extent that the 'Finance' solution had been adopted by one plant and the 'Production' solution by another. It appeared that the 'Production' solution was likely to be the one adopted throughout the organisation in the long term because of the political power of the department.

Attitudes towards training

With one exception training programmes for supervisors lasted for between two and three hours and were concerned predominantly with the technical aspects of operating the system. Both managers and supervisors were disinclined to make use of longer training programmes, but for different reasons. Managers, when asked, would relate the standard reasons of not being able to spare their supervisors to go on training courses and being unable to bear the costs of such exercises. In a period when staff were being cut it was very difficult for a training department to argue against the logic being put forward by line managers no matter what the strength of their cases. The one exception to this was in 'Components' which was a 'green field' site allowing time for supervisory training before the system was introduced.

Supervisors were often not motivated to go on training courses, particularly where they perceived them as 'remedial', as something to put 'right' what they had been doing 'wrong' for perhaps 20 years or more. Others have noted that supervisors can regard training as like 'going back to school' (Warr and Bird, 1976). The personal characteristics of some supervisors presented their own training obstacles. Many of the supervisors in the cases we studied were of an age and learning ability which made it more difficult for them to be trained successfully. This perhaps explains the hesitation of some managers to allow supervisors to input directly into the system. In the words of one manager 'men's wages are very sensitive and we don't want amateurs messing around'.

Reactions of supervisors

There were very few instances of outright opposition from supervisors towards the changes in technology; indeed, such a reaction could be counter-productive. In 'Hightech' the timekeepers took strike action following the breakdown of negotiations over a regrading claim resulting from the technical change. The strike lasted for six weeks during which time members of management ran a skeleton crew. This meant that manual employees received only their basic wage since it was not possible to calculate overtime and bonus pay. Subsequently, there was considerable pressure from the manual trade unions for the timekeepers to settle.

There were cases, however, of resistance to change, particularly where the MTR systems were linked to production control and loading packages particularly where 'the supervisors' skills of fixing and by-passing the formal system through a mixture of experience, cunning, personal contacts and trading of favours or indulgences, could appear to count for nought over-night' (Rothwell, 1984, p. 23). Commonly supervisors knew what was required of them but were disinclined to use the new technology, blaming technical and access problems. Supervisors would often ignore the facilities offered by the new techniques and maintain or modify the established customs and practices. In 'Luxury Goods' supervisors chose not to use the information system for making manning decisions, relying instead of the established 'swop' arrangements known to their bosses. The supervisors had usually worked out their own configurations, matching what was really needed against their own skills and abilities to cope (Rothwell and Davidson, 1983, p. 119). Some supervisors would attempt to demonstrate the distinctiveness of their skills and knowledge by by-passing the system and feeding in data which they knew were incorrect, resulting in 'garbage in, garbage out'.

These attitudes on the part of supervisors were sometimes encouraged by those around them, particularly their bosses. Managers themselves may be disinclined to use the new technology. Following the spectacular crash of the system in 'Assembly' its credibility in the eyes of managers was at rock bottom. The use of the technology could lead to increased work for managers. In 'Luxury Goods' where the information system gave managers access to manning figures they could, if they wished, decide on transfers of men. However, most supervisors were aware that the likely response from managers to their request to find more men if they were undermanned would be 'find them your ——— self'.

CONCLUSIONS

This chapter has looked at the changes introduced into supervisors' jobs and their training and development implications as part of a wider study of working arrangements associated with new time recording techniques. We argue that supervisors' jobs change in different ways and reject the idea that either a strengthening of weakening of supervisory discretion is in any way the inevitable result of technical change.

Three different changes in supervisors' jobs were observed: in two cases ('Hightech' and 'Consumer Products') managers sought to strengthen the role of the supervisor; in 'Assembly' and 'Luxury Goods' the aim appears to have been to weaken supervisory discretion; while in 'Components' greater authority and accountability went hand in hand. These variations can be traced back not simply to the characteristics of the technology itself but principally to the decisions made by managers on the design, implementation and operation of the new techniques.

The key issue therefore is the degree to which these decisions are implicit or explicit and involve supervisors themselves. Supervisors represent one of the key political groups in the change process and they are likely to be concerned about the impact of technical change on their executive, supervisory and disciplinary roles. However, supervisors are rarely involved in strategic decisions on new technology. Managerial practice in our case studies followed fairly closely the model put forward by Senker (1985) whereby top managers decide to introduce the new techniques and only later give thought to the repercussions.

Adopting this approach can have two consequences: senior managers will often be ignorant of time recording customs and practices and therefore inappropriate techniques are selected, and supervisors and middle managers may be reluctant to operate the new techniques in the way intended partly because of their doubts about the benefits of MTR systems. If the political nature of technical change is acknowledged the interests of the various competing interest groups affected will be identified. The opportunity then exists to take account of these in a systematic review of current supervisory practice and to consider how the supervisor might be developed to cope with future needs. Once this has been decided managers can then consider what technical changes and training programmes are needed to support the new supervisory role.

REFERENCES AND FURTHER READING

Arthurs, A. and Kinnie, N. (1984) 'Time Up for Clocking?', *Employee Relations*, 6, 4, pp. 22–5
——— (1986) 'New Techniques for Monitoring and Controlling Employee Activity at Work', in T. Lupton (ed.), *Human Factors in Manufacturing*, IFS Conferences, Bedford
Bessant, J. (1983) 'Management and Manufacturing Innovation: the case of information technology' in G. Winch (ed.), *Information Technology and Manufacturing Processes*, Rossendale, pp. 14–30

Bowey, A. (1973) 'The Changing Status of the Supervisor', *British Journal of Industrial Relations*, XI, 3, pp. 393–414

Brown, W. (1962) *Piecework Abandoned*, Heinemann, London

Buchanan, D. (1983) 'Technological Imperatives and Strategic Choice', in G. Winch (ed.), *Information Technology and Manufacturing Processes*, Rossendale, London, pp. 72–80

—— and Boddy, D. (1983) *Organisations in the Computer Age: Technological Imperatives and Strategic Choice*, Gower, Aldershot

Child, J. (1972) 'Organization Structure, Environment and Performance: The Role of Strategic Choice', *Sociology*, 6, 1, pp. 1–22

—— and Partridge, B. (1982) *Lost Managers*, Cambridge University Press, Cambridge

Davis, L.E. and Taylor, I.C. (1976) 'Technology organization and job structure', in R. Dubin (ed.), *Handbook of Work, Organization and Society*, Rand McNally, Chicago

Dawson, P. and McLoughlin, I. (1986) 'Computer Technology and the Redefinition of Supervision, : A Study of the Effects of Computerization on Railway Freight Supervisors', *Journal of Management Studies*, 23, 1, pp. 116–32

Dunkerley, D. (1975) *The Foreman*, Routledge & Kegan Paul, London

Fudge, C. (1986) 'Retraining for new technology: six success stories', *Personnel Management*, February, pp. 42–5

Kinnie, N. (1986) 'Introducing Information Technology into British Industry — the case of time recording equipment', End of Contract Report to the ESRC

—— and Arthurs, A. (1986) 'Clock, Clock — Who's there?', *Personnel Management*, August, pp. 40–6

Leavitt, H.J. and Whisler, T.L. (1958) 'Management in the 80's', *Harvard Business Review*, 36, 6, pp. 41–8

Piercy, N. (ed.) (1984) *The Management Implications of New Information Technology*, Croom Helm, London

Rajan, A. (1985) *Training and Recruitment Implications of Technical Change*, Gower, Aldershot

Rothwell, S. (1984) 'Supervisors and New Technology', *Employment Gazette*, January, pp. 21–5

—— and Davidson, D. (1983) 'Training for New Technology', in G. Winch (ed.) *Information Technology and Manufacturing Processes*, Rossendale, London, pp. 112–25

Senker, P. (1984) 'Training for Automation', in M. Warner (ed.), *Microprocessors, Manpower and Society*, Gower, Aldershot, pp. 134–46

—— (ed.) (1985) *Planning for Microelectronics in the Workplace*, Gower, Aldershot

—— and Beesley, M. (1985) 'Computerised Production and Inventory Control Systems: some skill and employment implications', *Industrial Relations Journal*, 16, 3, pp. 52–7

Sorge, A. and Warner, M. (1980) 'Manufacturing Organisation and Workplace Relations in Great Britain and West Germany', *British Journal of Industrial Relations*, XVIII, 3, pp. 318–33

Thurley, K. and Wirdenius, H. (1973) *Supervision: a Reappraisal*,

Heinemann, London

Walters, B. (1983) 'Identifying Training Needs', in D. Guest and T.A. Kenny, *Textbook of Techniques and Strategies in Personnel Management*, IPM, London

Warr, P.B. and Bird, M. (1976) *Identifying Supervisory Training Needs*, HMSO, London

Wilkinson, B. (1983) *The Shop Floor Politics of New Technology*, Gower, Aldershot

Winch, G. (ed.) (1983) *Information Technology and Manufacturing Processes*, Rossendale, London

Woodward, J. (1980) *Industrial Organization: Theory and Practice*, 2nd edn, Oxford University Press, London

11

Towards a New Framework for Helping Managers to Deal with Technical Change

David Boddy

This chapter outlines a method we have developed to help managers and project staff to deal more confidently with the issues raised by the availability of computing and information technology. Our own earlier studies, like those of many other researchers, have shown clearly that the results of investing in information technology depend on how a wide range of management and organisational issues are dealt with. This conclusion appeared to have potential practical value to those charged with introducing computing and information technology. We therefore decided to produce a practical technique which would support their efforts. This chapter outlines the origins of the idea; the organisational actors for whom it is intended; how we developed it; and the main features of the finished work.

CONCEPT

More than 30 years after computers began to become widely available, the belief continues to be expressed that computers in themselves have an independent effect on events. An awareness of the growing technical sophistication of available equipment appears to lead to this view. Computer-aided equipment is often sold on that basis, in the sense that much publicity implies that computers will solve organisational or managerial problems. In other contexts, anxieties often stem from the same perception, in the sense that computers are seen as a cause of unemployment or a loss of identity at work.

This deterministic view is mistaken and can only be supported by a selective interpretation of events or by heavy extrapolation from narrowly defined units of analysis. A view much more in line with the evidence is that which stresses the role of human choice in determining the consequences of computer-aided equipment.

For example, in 1966 Jay Forester, concluding a conference on the impact of computers on management, commented as follows:

> I see data processing as opening a fork in the road. Most organizations in the short run will choose the path to greater centralization . . . The other road leads to new types of organization, [and to] new concepts of corporate government . . . The choice is before us; the path is not determined by the nature of electronic computers (Forester, 1967).

This theme of choice was further developed by writers such as Walton (1982), Sorge *et al.* (1983) and Wilkinson (1983). Our own studies (Buchanan and Boddy, 1983; Boddy and Buchanan, 1986) are consistent with this view. We have studied many different applications of computer technology, such as word processing in office systems; computer numerically controlled machine tools; computer-aided process control; computer-aided reservation systems in hotels; and computer-aided laboratory systems in hospitals. These studies have involved detailed examinations of actual installations, gathering documentary evidence, talking to managers, project staff and operators, as well as to those indirectly affected.

The common theme to emerge from this empirical work has been that the results obtained, whether or not they were in line with initial expectations, were associated not only with the technical or other qualities of the equipment, but with a host of other decisions that were taken, or other events which occurred, in the course of the computer project. This led us to the view that technology in itself neither solved problems, not created them.

The availability of computing and information technology in the market merely triggered a decision process within organisations, about whether to make use of that capability, and if so how to make use of it. The latter set of decisions included not just technical options, though clearly they were important. They also included such matters as the way in which work was to be organised, how procedures for controlling the flow of work were to be reshaped, changes in structure and in the role of management, and the way in which the projects themselves were managed. Within each of these broad areas, many specific operational choices were made by those with a responsibility for the project.

125

The choices that were made on these matters, either consciously or unconsciously, and the particular context in which they were taken, had influenced the attitudes and behaviour of those organisational members with a stake in the project. The decisions had affected people's attitudes towards the technology and towards their overall status in, and commitment to, the organisation. In some cases these choices had produced positive effects and had enabled the technology to contribute dramatically to the fortunes of the organisation. In other cases, the decisions had produced attitudes amongst staff such that the technology appeared, objectively, to be something of an expensive embarrassment.

Research conclusions such as these are, we hope, a useful contribution to the work of the social sciences in understanding significant social processes. They also appeared to have practical value to those organisational members directly involved in such processes. Our work as management teachers encouraged us to develop this research into a form that would meet their needs.

CUSTOMERS

In producing a decision guide, we have concentrated on those in the organisation who are likely to have the most active role in the overall management of an information technology project, namely the 'promoter' and the 'internal consultant'. The vital position of the promoter or champion has long been recognised in studies of technical change, the term being applied to the person who initiates or takes over an idea and turns it into operating reality. They will usually be from 'user' departments and will often be referred to as the project leader. The internal consultant role is also likely to be important during information technology projects, which often require technical computing or systems advice. They will usually be technical experts from computing or management services departments. We recognise that others such as users or user management will also have significant roles, but our principal focus is on the promoters or project leaders, and on internal consultants.

The situation we perceived was that project leaders or promoters from the functional area into which technology was being introduced typically had little systematic experience or knowledge of other computer projects. They were, therefore, unlikely to be aware of the range of issues which would need to be dealt with (many of which they already deal with anyway in their daily management capacity), and could thus lose this opportunity to influence the project outcome. Systems specialists (the internal consultants) tend, quite naturally, to deal only with technical issues, being neither aware of nor competent to deal with the broader management issues. There is thus a danger of both groups operating without obtaining the benefits of the experience which could be obtained from previous installations. We therefore decided to produce a decision guide which would help to overcome this difficulty. Financial support was obtained from the Manpower Services Commission and the process of development began which is described in the next section.

CREATION

From our earlier research, we had developed a broad view of the issues which had affected the outcomes of computer projects, and with which the staff needed to deal. As indicated above, these were in such areas as clarifying objectives, selecting equipment, deciding on work organisation, and so on. However, they were still expressed at a rather general level and had not been subject to systematic scrutiny. We were not confident that they adequately reflected the full range of issues with which project staff had to deal, nor that they were expressed in sufficiently specific operational detail. This latter point was important, as project staff are usually quite well aware of the 'issues' — what they seek is guidance on how to deal with them. Nor were we confident at the outset of the project as to the best way to package the issues and decisions, in a way that would be usable by those who were grappling, under pressure, with novel and possibly controversial projects. We therefore engaged in three principal activities.

First, we conducted an Information Technology Learning Programme. This was attended over a nine-month period by project staff from twelve organisations, each engaged in a major information technology project. They attended the business school for one day each month. For about half of each day they worked in small groups, outlining to each other the progress which they had made on their respective projects, and receiving advice, comments and questions from the other members of their group. They then produced individual action plans for the subsequent period, and recorded the major issues which were currently of concern to members of the group. The other half of each day was taken up with presentations from the staff on issues with which we had been working, and with work on diagnostic exercises which we had been creating.

This programme proved outstandingly valuable to the project. In part, it confirmed that the issues with which we were dealing were also the concern of the companies represented. It also, as we had hoped, added to the range of issues with which the decision guide would have to deal. For example, the group's discussion drew our attention to important choices which had arisen in their projects in areas such as corporate responsibility for computing; the phasing and planning of projects; the importance of selling projects to senior management; and the problems of creating good relations with suppliers.

The second major activity, which we were conducting in parallel with the learning programme, was to develop practical means of bringing the issues to the attention of project staff, and of supporting their unique decision processes. We took the view that the issues would be most acceptable if presented in many small, distinct sections, rather than as conventional chapters dealing with a range of issues. Each such section would be only four or five pages long, and would consist, typically, of a brief note on the issue, one or two practical examples of how the issue had been dealt with (successfully or unsuccessfully); some checklists of questions to ask; and perhaps some diagnostic tools.

Our main model for the latter was the extensive work which had already been done in the field of management and organisation development to develop diagnostic tools and instruments. These have been widely used on general management programmes with considerable success and we felt that they provided a useful approach to enabling staff to deal with the issued raised by new technology.

Third, we have been testing these instruments as they have been developed. An obvious place was of course the ITLP itself, where, as we have already indicated, about half of each session was spent on presentations from ourselves and on working through the materials and exercises we were developing. For example, if it was decided to spend some time on objective setting then we presented our ideas on the topic, and gave the participants an individual and perhaps a group exercise on which to work. That not only identified and clarified some issues to do with objective setting, but also helped us to identify the strengths and weaknesses in the exercises themselves.

In addition, we have used the materials successfully on our own university postgraduate management courses, and on some programmes which we have been invited to run for other organisations. This process of testing has in itself not only improved the materials themselves, but has been a further way of clarifying the issues with which those taking part in such programmes were having to deal.

CONTENT

In the course of developing the framework, our initial set of areas of decision was expanded and reformulated many times, as it was tested against the experience of those with whom we worked on the ITLP, on our courses, and against the issues emerging in the other research projects which we were conducting at the same time. We also felt that one feature of the workbook, if it was to be useful, should be that it would have a clear, easily remembered structure. This conflict between comprehensiveness and parsimony has been resolved by grouping the range of decisions into a simple organising framework, consisting of three large modules, each of which contains three smaller sections, which in turn contains four or five specific topics. In addition, there are two preliminary modules which set the scene and give some guidance on how to use the material.

At the broadest level the material is organised as shown in Figure 11.1. This reflects our position that the results obtained from investing in new technology depends on the decisions which are made in these three broad areas of Purpose, People and the Process.

Within each of the three blocks, there are three units. Their titles and their overall message are as follows:

PURPOSE

Strategic focus   Ensure that the use of new technology has a clear strategic focus which targets long-term market objectives and not just current internal operating problems.

Positive policies   Review and implement positive policies in areas like employment practice and investment appraisal, so that they encourage innovation and the strategic use of new technology.

Kit to fit   When evaluating hardware and software options, make sure that you choose kit to fit the current and anticipated needs of the business.

Figure 11.1: The RAP3 process

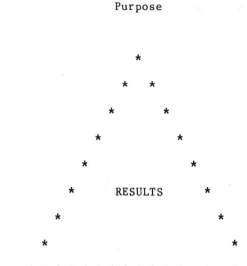

Purpose

RESULTS

People * * * * * * * * * * * * * * * * * Process

PEOPLE

Work organisation   Review work organisation in relation to new technology, to encourage flexibility, creativity and skills development.

Support systems   Design support systems which are consistent with strategic aims, and which enable support staff to contribute in flexible and creative ways to the changing needs of the organisation.

Management styles   Review management styles and working arrangements, to ensure that these are consistent with the strategic goals of the business, and with achieving the potential benefits of new technology.

PROCESS

Project manage-
ment   Establish a clear project management responsibility to guide the often protracted implementation process.

Involvement   Plan the nature and timing of user involvement,

130

to ensure that key staff establish 'ownership' of new equipment and procedures.

Competence   Develop a systematic training plan to equip users at all levels with the competence, in the form of new skills and knowledge, they need to exploit the innovative potential of the new technology.

Each of the nine modules contains four or five individual sections, each dealing with a particular topic. As an example, the section on work organisation includes the following topics:

— Organising Individual Jobs
— Organising Jobs into Groups
— A Strategy for Organising Work
— Winning Acceptance of Change

As well as trying to include a comprehensive view of the areas of choice in the workbook, we are also aware that it needs to recognise the reality of decision-making in organisations, which is generally far removed from being an orderly objective process. The workbook recognises that the individual using the workbook is one among many stakeholders, and that as well as introducing the project successfully they will have their own interests to pursue and their own position to defend. It recognises the political element in organisational change and also the specific roles which someone using it is likely to have to exercise.

CONCLUSIONS

Three lessons stand out when we review our experience of this project. First, the managers and professional staff who worked with us were very receptive to the concept and method of approach. They were well aware from their own direct experience that major technical changes needed to be accompanied by appropriate organisational changes, if the full benefits were to be achieved. They had seen both successful and unsuccessful projects, and had been able to relate these outcomes to the extent to which managements had been able and willing to act on all dimensions of the project, rather than acting only on the technical dimension.

Second, while they were aware of the issues which needed to be

131

addressed by the researchers and by other managers, they were much less confident as to what to do about the issues. They were keen to get examples of experience elsewhere, to get checklists or frameworks to assess their own situation, and to seek reassurance that a course of action they proposed was along the right lines. They were especially interested in the problem of how best to make a case for action to senior management, thereby recognising that successful technical change depends heavily on the skilful influence of those higher up the organisation.

Finally, there was wide support for the view that those who really determine the success or otherwise of a technical change are the senior management of the area concerned. Numerous examples were quoted of ways in which senior management decisions affected the results. These cover such matters as how computing responsibilities were allocated; the resources allocated to information technology; senior management awareness of strategic *and* technical issues; the kind of investment appraised procedures used; and policies on payment systems and working arrangements. In cases where senior management had dealt appropriately with these areas, projects were generally successful; while unsuccessful projects stemmed from organisational policies which encouraged a short-term, technical focus, unrelated to broader business concerns. Perhaps the emphasis should now be on the implications for training and development of senior managers, if their companies are to make best use of the available technologies.

REFERENCES

Boddy, D. and Buchanan, D.A. (1986) *Managing New Technology*, Basil Blackwell, Oxford

Buchanan, D.A. and Boddy, D. (1983) *Organizations in the Computer Age : Technological Imperatives and Strategic Choice*, Gower, Aldershot

Forester, Jay W. (1967) 'Comments on the conference discussion proceedings', in C.A. Myers (ed.), *The Impact of Computers on Management*, MIT Press, Cambridge, Mass.

Sorge, A., Hartmann, G., Warner, M. and Nicholas, I. (1983) *Microelectronics and Manpower in Manufacturing*, Gower, Aldershot

Walton, R.E. (1982) 'Social Choice in the Development of Advanced Information Technology', *Human Relations*, 35, pp. 1073–84

Wilkinson, B. (1983) *The Shop Floor Politics of New Technology*, Gower, Aldershot

12

Developing Managers to Meet the New Challenges

David Boddy and David Buchanan

This final chapter sets out the management development implications of the experiences with information technologies which have been described earlier. Drawing on this evidence, what kinds of development are needed, if the challenges we have identified are to be met? In particular, what do managers need to be able to do better if the huge sums spent on computer projects are to bring about demonstrable improvements in the performance of managers, and of their organisations?

MONITORING AND CONTROLLING PERFORMANCE

The chapters dealing with changes in the monitoring and controlling roles of managers indicated some very clear development needs. In Chapter 2, for example, it was argued that in order to make use of the information now becoming available through information systems, managers needed to have enhanced system knowledge, more ability to specify information needs, and greater interpretive skills. The first of these refers to the need to be able to take an informed and critical view of information, based on a thorough understanding of and 'feel' for the primary sources of the data, and the processing to which they have been subject. A feature of recent computer development has been the growth in the ability of systems to capture and process data at the time of the original transaction, without the need for further human intervention. Done well, this can greatly enhance the insight a manager already familiar with basic operations can have for events. The danger lies in over-reliance on information which is based on keys pressed by a busy clerk or waitress in a remote location, who perhaps themselves had little appreciation of (or interest in) the uses to which the processed data would be put.

The need for managers to improve their ability to specify information needs was also raised in Chapters 3, 4 and 5. One of the reasons why managers in Martin's sample (Chapter 3) discontinued their use of computers, even after they had invested a lot of effort in learning to use them, was that the systems were not attuned to the kind of information they needed. Martin proposed that this put a new onus on software designers to come up with more appropriate systems: for that to work requires a prior activity to ensure that managers are able to express their information needs adequately. Barbara Rawlings also drew attention to this point in her discussion of the 'knowledge gap' between managers and computer specialists. A valuable point in her discussion was the warning that, unless properly dealt with through a development activity, this gap could grow wider as a project progresses.

A warning of the inherent difficulties to be overcome in such an activity is given in Arjen Wassenaar's account in Chapter 5 of the introduction of a computer-integrated manufacturing project. He found that managers experienced severe difficulties in concepts of information management, such as 'information, data, data models, entities, structuring of data, etc.'. In addition, and much harder to change, he concluded that 'Managers prefer to think in authority lines and vertical information systems. Structured horizontal information flows crossing the borders of their areas of authority were a rather unknown issue in their work' (p. 54). Yet without that, he argued, they were unable to make full use of the potential benefits of the new information system.

The need for greater interpretive ability grows with the amount of information available to managers. It is wrong to assume that because managers are appearing to use a system, they are actually using it effectively: the chances are that, without appropriate training, it will be significantly under-used.

Chapter 4 by Douglas Macbeth raised a fundamental question which needs to be thought through, namely, whether managers want to follow the 'high-tech' route to monitor and control activities, or whether they would be better off with a well-designed 'low-tech' solution. Drawing on Schonberger (1986), he described how in some 'state of the art' plants much information is localised, and confined to the areas where it can be used: for example statistical process control charts or graphs of improvement patterns are held only at the place of operation, and not transmitted electronically to

Figure 12.1: The IT balancing act

Benefits	Problems
more information quicker information better decision	pressure to respond visibility heightened stress

senior managers: if they want to know what is happening they come and look.

Given the pressure from the computer industry towards ever more sophisticated 'high-tech' solutions, a pressing development need is to remind managers that 'low-tech' solutions can be productive, and may, in appropriate circumstances, also be a better basis for monitoring and controlling performance.

It is important to highlight this choice, because it is becoming very clear that sophisticated information technology systems can bring threats as well as benefits, as shown in Figure 12.1. The benefits of additional, more timely information are frequently expressed: the possible threats are rather less often considered. The extra pressure to respond to information may lead to erratic, over-involved management; the greater visibility of performance can lead to heightened stress and worse performance; managers need then to balance the benefits and the risks of using ever more sophisticated technical solutions to the problems of monitoring and controlling performance: and an awareness that low-tech solutions exist and can work widens the decision space.

GIVING DIRECTION AND PURPOSE

Information technology also poses a challenge to managers in their role of giving direction and purpose to the organisation. The chapters by Wassenaar, Macbeth and Rawlings each gave insight into this challenge, and into its development implications. Wassenaar showed that implementing new technology in what he called the 'primary business function' not only meant changes to work structures, but also led to a greater emphasis on horizontal rather than

135

vertical flows of information. Managers found this difficult to visualise; perhaps because of their current operating emphasis, they found it hard to see the links between new technology and strategy.

Macbeth too showed how manufacturing processes need to be seen as an integral part of an organisation's strategy. Drawing on Skinner (1969), he reminded us that if decisions or facilities are delegated to operating staff, directions may be taken which, while apparently correct to middle management, may not be consistent with strategic policies. This remains true as choices arise over the way new information technologies are used to support manufacturing.

From both chapters, it is clear that a major development issue is to ensure that senior managers have sufficient technical awareness to be able to see the strategic possibilities of their manufacturing operation. As well as this technical awareness, Wassenaar showed how different thinking styles were needed, together with greater skill and willingness to plan innovation in conjunction with managers from other functional groups.

The same kind of need was evident in Barbara Rawlings' chapter. She gave an example of how the knowledge gap between managers and computer experts could widen, rather than diminish, in the course of a project. Clearly, inadequate technical awareness makes it impossible for senior managers to see the strategic possibilities of information technology.

It is important too that managers recognise the risks of adopting a strategic approach to information technology. Although the benefits can be open-ended, so can the costs. There are high risks in going for fully integrated systems — especially if the business then becomes dependent on them. And given the rapidity of change, there are risks attached to a strategy that closes off some options. In establishing direction, these risks need to be set against the potential benefits of linking technical developments closely to business strategy.

CHANGING ORGANISATION STRUCTURE

The final challenge posed for managers by new technology is whether, and how, to change the organisation structure. In some cases the challenge concerned how best to reorganise computing facilities, in others the issue was the balance between centralised and decentralised decision-making, while in others again it concerned changes in the role of supervisors. Training of supervisors in the requirements of their changing roles was proposed by Dawson and McLoughlin without which they implied supervisors would become progressively marginal. The problems which inadequate training would cause were indicated by Kinnie and Arthurs, who pointed out that, while senior managers establish the broad direction of change, the burden of implementing it falls on middle managers and supervisors.

More broadly, managers need the opportunity to enhance their skills of changing aspects of organisation structures in conjunction with changes in technology. Technical change, together with greater market uncertainly, requires more flexible working arrangements, and a more effective use of assets. Many established organisational designs do not respond easily to market, product and technical changes, and do not stimulate high motivation and commitment from employees. Managers need a greater awareness of the alternatives that are available, and a greater confidence to begin experimenting with such alternatives. Concepts such as autonomous team working, for example, are highly relevant to the effective introduction of technical change, and managers need a greater awareness of such concepts, and of how to implement them in practice.

Large-scale change carries with it significant risks. It takes up significant amounts of management time, may arouse suspicion, animosity or outright opposition, and may be highly disruptive to current operations. Moreover, those proposing or implementing such changes place themselves in a highly exposed position, where people will be very willing to remember their mistakes, while successes are taken for granted. Proposing such changes, as well as major technical changes, places a manager in an uncomfortably vulnerable position.

We hope this book will help managers, and those who work with them, to deal more confidently with that vulnerable position, and will encourage them to take a proactive, rather than a reactive, role towards information technology. The common theme throughout this book has been the choices which technology opens up for managers, in their roles of monitoring performance, setting direction, and changing structures. The key challenge is to balance the opportunities and risks opened up by the technology in a way which will improve business performance. That will only happen if managers realise that technology does not determine events, but merely opens up choices.

FUTURE RESEARCH

Finally, what do the chapters in this book suggest as the most urgent research topics? It is clear that a strong research activity has developed around the organisational and human aspects of information technology, but two features are conspicuous by their absence.

The first is the relatively limited amount of comparative study between different countries in Europe. There have been some very useful comparative studies such as those by Sorge *et al.* (1983), but they are rare. Given the scope for choice in application which information technology provides, and given the differences in national cultures which guide those choices, more comparative studies of the implementation of similar technologies are overdue. They would provide a rich source of ideas on the range of options available, and further emphasise the non-determinist nature of these technologies.

Second, it would be of great practical value to find out more about the circumstances in which more information leads to better management decisions. There are cases where a clear link can be shown between the introduction of information technology, more informed management decisions, and a measurable improvement in some performance indicators. Equally, however, there are cases where, when pressed, it has been difficult for managers to show these links with any conviction. And there is a view that information (especially if it is emanating from a costly high-tech terminal) can be used as a ritual, for the sake of appearance, or as a confidence-building exercise.

The actual strength of the links between information availability and management performance is relevant whatever the system discussed. It becomes more urgent as the convergence of computing and telecommunication technologies make possible dramatic increases in the quantity, and of course in the cost, of the information available to managers. Knowing more clearly how such systems in practice bring tangible benefits to individuals and organisations would further clarify the true nature of the new management challenge.

REFERENCES

Schonberger, R.J. (1986), *World Class Manufacturing: The Lessons of Simplicity Applied*, Free Press, New York

Skinner, W. (1969), 'Manufacturing — Missing Link in Corporate

Strategy', *Harvard Business Review*, May–June, pp. 136–49

Sorge, A., Hartmann, G., Warner, M. and Nicholas, L. (1983) *Micro-electronics and Manpower in Manufacturing*, Gower, Aldershot

Index